Official The THREE STOOGES COOKBOOK ™

Robert Kurson

CB
CONTEMPORARY BOOKS

Library of Congress Cataloging-in-Publication Data

Kurson, Robert.
      The official Three Stooges cookbook / Robert Kurson.
        p.   cm.
      ISBN 0-8092-2929-3
        1. Cookery, American.   2. Three Stooges (Comedy team)   I. Title.
      TX715.K938   1998
      641.5973—dc21   98-25741
                                                                          CIP

For Amy, whose home cooking, gentle presence, and unconditional support nourish me constantly

"The Three Stooges"™ and "Knuckleheads"™ are trademarks of Comedy III Productions, Inc. The Three Stooges characters, names, and all related indicia are trademarks of Comedy III Productions, Inc.

Cover design by Todd Petersen
Interior design by Hespenheide Design
Cover and interior photographs courtesy Comedy III Productions, Inc.

Published by Contemporary Books
A division of NTC/Contemporary Publishing Group, Inc.
4255 West Touhy Avenue, Lincolnwood (Chicago), Illinois 60646-1975 U.S.A.
Copyright © 1999 by Comedy III Productions, Inc.
Printed in the United States of America
International Standard Book Number: 0-8092-2929-3
98 99 00 01 02 03 QD 18 17 16 15 14 13 12 11 10 9 8 7 6 5 4 3 2 1

Contents

3
Beverages

4
Breakfast

5
Snacks

6
Lunch

7
Soups and Salads

8
Dinner

9
Desserts

Acknowledgments

The author would like to thank the following people for their kind, generous, and often yummy contributions to this book:

Annette Kurson, both the finest writer and the best cook I know. Her prose is rivaled only by her lasagna.

Ken and Becky Kurson—Ken for his deft hand in guiding my pen, Becky for her support, encouragement, and all those exquisite tacos.

Mike, Sam, Jane, and Larry Glover, a family from whom I get constant encouragement, wonderful recipes, and an endless supply of delicious, home-cooked dinners.

> **Woman:** Do you have a haddock?
> **Curly:** No, I don't have no haddock, but I get a little attack here every time I eat too much.
> *Cookoo Cavaliers*

Jack Kurson, who made it a pleasure to wake up early on Saturday mornings not only to watch the Stooges, but to watch him watch the Stooges.

My aunts, uncles, and cousins in the Jacobs and Weiss families, who have watched me grow from Stooge fan to Stooge author to the pinnacle of success—Stooge cook.

Cousins Sam Zell, Jeff Zell, and Allen Weingarten, who reenacted Stooge bits with me even when I was too young to understand why "Marshmallow Gumbo" was funny.

Harry and Helen Jacobs, world-class cooks who did it all by feel.

Robert Feder, Elliott Harris, and Bob Mazzoni—three of the best riveters who ever riveted . . . wait . . . three of the best friends and colleagues a guy could have.

Nigel Wade and Larry Green, my bosses at the *Chicago Sun-Times*, who believed in me and gave me a chance.

Nancy Cassman, Paige Smoron, Henry Kisor, Neil Steinberg, Jae-Ha Kim, Rich Roeper, Phil Rosenthal, John Barron, and my colleagues in the Features department at the *Chicago Sun-Times*; their brainstorming sessions were food for the funnybone.

Craig Bolt, Maureen Musker, Christine Albritton, and Matthew Carnicelli at Contemporary Books for their patience, easy touch, and friendship; they make an author's job fun.

Bela G. Lugosi, Kathy, Arlene, and everyone at Comedy III Productions for their constant spirit of teamwork.

Harry Ross, Stooge fan extraordinaire and a genuine nice guy.

Andrew, Jeannie, and Alec Beresin, without whom these books would have stayed just a great idea.

Pals Jason Steigman, Mitch Cassman, Rich Hanus, Ken Goldin, Barry Codell, Jeff Lescher, Ken Andre, Jordan Heller, Brad Ginsberg, and Randi Lipin for making my days fun and challenging and providing me with so many laughs.

Brother Eric Davis, who loves to eat nearly as much as he loves the Stooges.

Bill Gilger, a buddy whose kindness and selflessness I won't forget.

Finally, my agent, the tireless and protective Shari Lesser Wenk; what a long, strange trip it's been!

> **Larry:** Why don't we get out of this restaurant business anyway?
>
> **Moe (impatient):** Why don't catfish have kittens?
>
> **Larry (hand on chin, looking skyward, perplexed):** I wonder . . .
>
> *Playing the Ponies*

Introduction

If you want to cook, go to the source: the Three Stooges.

The Stooges are always cooking: Roast turkeys that squawk when carved. Clams that bite. Filet of Sole and Heel.

Watch the Stooges and you'll begin to crave burned toast and a rotten egg. You'll splash whipped cream on your bologna. You'll eat the peel, not the banana.

World cuisine continues to be influenced by the Stooges. In many countries, pies are now baked strictly for throwing, while limburger—the Stooges' cheese of choice—has exploded in smelly popularity. Every French chef now prepares Cackle Soup the way Curly did, by pouring boiling water into a skinny chicken, wringing its legs, and delightedly singing "La-lee, La-la lee."

> "You never eat peas with a knife. You mix 'em with the mashed potatoes . . . then you eat 'em with a spoon."
> Moe to Curly in *Half-Wits Holiday*

> **Larry (horrified):** My lamb chop lost his pants!
> **Moe:** Well, dress him and eat him.
> *Half-Wits Holiday*

This cookbook stirs together all that is delicious in Stooge films. Some recipes, such as Cackle Soup, Roast Stooge, and Filet of Sole and Heel, are actually prepared by the Stooges in their films. Others, such as Sloppy Moes, Porcupine Potatoes, and Curly Fries are inspired by their hilarious relationship with food. With practice, you might even decide to open a

Moe (trying to fasten belt around Curly's waist): Now, if you didn't have T.B., I'd be able to get this around you.

Curly: What do you mean, T.B.?

Moe: Two bellies!

Three Smart Saps

"We'll cook you a dinner that'll be the talk of the town . . . and the county, too!"

Curly, *An Ache in Every Stake*

restaurant like the Stooge-owned Flounder Inn.

Each recipe is rated for difficulty using an actual insult hurled by Moe. Along the way, you'll find hilarious Stooge quotes about food ("Are you casting asparagus on my cooking?") and lots of funny food features, such as the "Ten Commandments of Stooge Cooking" and "Stooge Songs to Cook By." You'll even discover how much Curly weighs!

Before this cookbook, it took years of careful observation to learn to cook like the Stooges. Now, even amateur Stooge lovers can prepare masterpieces like Limburger à la Larry and Southern Comforter in less time than it takes to burn a turkey.

Congratulations, food connoisseurs and would-be chefs—you're about to learn to cook like a Stooge.

The Ten Commandments of Stooge Cooking

● ● ● ● ● ● ● ● ● ● ● ● ● ●

Thou shalt flip food in a pan such that it sticketh to the ceiling or the face of thine friend.

Thou shalt not panic when thy baked turkey yelpeth loudly and walketh away from thy dinner table.

Thou shalt consume beverages in one swig and at maximum gulping volume.

Thou shalt look skyward and cackle loudly when preparing eggs.

Thou shalt stab or maim any sandwich that attempteth to bite thee.

Thou shalt mistake a friend's arm for luncheon meat and spread mustard on it accordingly.

Thou shalt mistakenly substitute a pot holder for pancakes in all recipes.

Thou shalt continue to add strength to thy mixed drinks until fireworks and smoke billow forth from thy goblet.

Thou shalt discard all stuffings from inside bananas, crabs, and lobsters, for they are verboten.

Thou shalt pile sandwiches so high that they reacheth unto Heaven.

Thou shalt use only the stalest of ingredients—and in bountiful amounts.

Chapter 1

Side Dishes

Curly Fries

Difficulty Level: Squashbrain

Curly fries are the latest dining rage. Mysteriously, Curly has been given little credit for the phenomenon.

The similarities between Curly and curly fries are staggering: both are oddly shaped, spicy, and composed mainly of fat. It is true that Curly sings delightful songs and performs expressive dances, while curly fries remain mostly silent. But all in all, it is clear that Curly deserves the credit for the rise of curly fries.

Don't count on corporate America to acknowledge that Curly inspired curly fries. Instead, prepare this recipe proudly and with a capital C, and remember that when it comes to receiving the credit he deserves, Curly has always been a victim of soicumstance.

....

1 pound frozen curly fries

1 cup pasteurized process cheese sauce

Paprika to taste

1. Preheat oven to 425°F. Place the frozen curly fries on a small baking sheet to fit in a single layer. Bake for 12 minutes, stirring once.

2. Spoon the cheese sauce evenly over the potatoes. Sprinkle with paprika, as desired.

3. Return the potatoes to the oven about 6 minutes longer, or until cheese is bubbling hot. Serve immediately.

Makes 4 servings

Stooge cooking flatters your figure.

Moe's Mashed Potatoes for Building Mashed Potato Muscles

Difficulty Level: General Nuisance

Moe's massive muscles make sense.

They allow him to poke effortlessly, pull hair without strain, pinch with the power of 1,000 men.

No one handed Moe his multitude of muscles. He had to earn them by lifting heavy weapons like wrenches and hammers, and by eating strongman foods like steak and mashed potatoes. You never saw Moe eat quiche.

If you want to walk around like a 98-pound weakling, skip this recipe and fix yourself some celery sticks. But for a bossy physique like Moe's, scoop up a triple helping of Moe's Mashed Potatoes for Building Mashed Potato Muscles . . . and get ready to call the shots.

"Oh, a clip joint!"
Curly, to a fancy party guest
after losing his watch in some mashed
potatoes in *An Ache in Every Stake*

· ·

2 pounds potatoes, scrubbed but not peeled

6 tablespoons butter

6 tablespoons milk

1 teaspoon salt

½ teaspoon freshly ground black pepper

1 12-ounce jar home-style
chicken or turkey gravy

1. Cut small potatoes in half, or quarter large potatoes. Put them into a pot and fill with cold water to cover potatoes by 2 inches. Add a little salt to the water and cover the pot. Bring the water to a boil, then reduce heat to low and simmer the potatoes until they are very tender, 15 to 20 minutes. Turn off the heat.

2. Combine the butter and milk in a mixing bowl. Scoop out ⅓ cup of the potato cooking water and add it to the bowl. Drain the potatoes, and add them to the bowl. Smash the potatoes with a hand-held potato masher until they are well blended but still slightly lumpy. Season with the salt and pepper.

3. Remove the lid of the gravy jar and cover it loosely with plastic wrap, or transfer the contents of the jar to a microwave-safe dish. Microwave the gravy on high until hot, 2 to 3 minutes, stirring once. Use a towel to remove the jar from the microwave because it will be too hot to touch. Spoon hot gravy onto each serving of mashed potatoes.

Makes 6 servings

Beans, Beans, Beans!

Difficulty Level: Beetlebrain

Prospective chefs should learn a lesson from Curly's experience with baked beans in *Back From the Front*: too much of even the finest food is not a good thing.

Curly has been ordered to clean the cannon on a gunboat, but he is famished. Moe and Larry have been spared such orders, and promise to smuggle lunch to their pal.

"Oh, boy!" Curly exclaims. "Make it turkey and ham and candied sweet potatoes on the side, and smother the whole thing in fried chicken. But no beans!"

Curly, it seems, has eaten nothing but beans for weeks. Soon Moe and Larry return with a plate of food.

"That's what I call a pal!" Curly says joyously. "Roast turkey, stuffed breast. Oh, I love it!"

But when Curly discovers that it's nothing but a plate of beans, his spirits sink.

"Beans! That's all I get is beans!" he squeals.

Prepare this recipe in small amounts. Otherwise, you might wind up very angry at a problem that should be just a hill of beans.

Stooges' Beans, Beans, Beans!

●●●

4 large cans baked beans

1 large cannon

1 plunger

Enlist in the navy. Get assigned to cannon cleaning detail. Disobey orders and eat baked beans while on duty. When bossy admiral approaches, panic and ditch beans in muzzle of cannon, then look innocent.

When officer demands to know whether you've cleaned the cannon, reply as Curly does in *Back From the Front* by saying, "I wouldn't be surprised!" After admiral looks inside cannon and yells, "This gun is filthy, I tell you; swab it out. Come on; when I ask for service, give it to me!" ram plunger into cannon and discharge beans into his face. Run.

Another Beans, Beans, Beans!

1 tablespoon bacon fat or lard

1 medium–small onion, chopped

1 28-ounce can baked beans

½ tablespoon Worcestershire sauce

½ tablespoon mustard

½ teaspoon hot sauce

1. In a medium cast-iron skillet, melt the fat over medium heat. Add the onion and cook, stirring occasionally, until it is soft and golden, about 10 minutes.

2. Add the baked beans and stir to mix with the onions. Stir in the Worcestershire sauce, mustard, and hot sauce. Continue to cook, stirring occasionally, until mixture is thick and tasty, about 10 minutes.

Makes 6 servings

Thunderbolt's Chili Pepperino Salsa

Difficulty Level: Half-Brother to a Weasel

What makes a racehorse run?

Some say genetics. Others claim that it's training. The Stooges know it's food. Spicy food.

Stuck with a broken-down nag named Thunderbolt in *Playing the Ponies*, Moe, Larry, and Curly seem ready to abandon the horse racing business when the easygoing nag takes a nibble of Curly's blazing hot chili pepperino snack.

Thunderbolt's personality changes rapidly. He rears up, blasts smoke from his nostrils, and neighs like a banshee. Then he takes off down the practice track as if propelled by twin rocket boosters. The Stooges realize that they are practically in the dough . . . if only they can figure out how to make Thunderbolt run in the right direction.

This recipe for Thunderbolt's Chili Pepperino Salsa is suitable for anyone who enjoys spicy food; it can also be financially rewarding for Olympic athletes and bank robbers. Those who intend to remain in one place, however, should apply the stuff sparingly—or risk ending up in the winner's circle at a nearby racetrack.

....

1 14½-ounce can diced tomatoes, drained

1 4-ounce can diced green chilies, drained

½ cup chopped onion

1 tablespoon hot sauce

1 teaspoon white vinegar

½ teaspoon salt

Combine all the ingredients in an electric blender or a food processor. Blend until ingredients are finely ground, but not liquefied. Pour the salsa into a jar, cover, and store in the refrigerator until ready to use.

Makes 1¾ cups salsa, about 6 servings

Curly's baby formula (100 proof).

Joe Strubachincoscow's Moscow Latkes

Difficulty Level: Overstuffed Bologna

Largely forgotten today, Joe Strubachincoscow influenced the development of early aviation in ways Orville and Wilbur never imagined.

As draft board officer for the Republic of Cannabeer, P.U., in *Dizzy Pilots*, Strubachincoscow warns the Wrong Brothers— Moe, Larry, and Curly—that they will be drafted into the army if construction on their revolutionary new airplane, the *Buzzard*, is not completed in 30 days.

Some consider Strubachincoscow's deadline unreasonable. But after seeing the *Buzzard* fly, even the staunchest Stooge fan must concede that the ground-based army is probably the safest place for the Wrong Brothers.

To honor Strubachincoscow's contributions to aviation safety, this special recipe was flown in from Moscow—in a fully licensed and inspected airplane. Just don't eat too many of the dense delicacies, or you'll wind up as grounded as the Wrong Brothers.

Moe: Hey, what's the idea of spreading mashed potatoes around on your bread? Why don't you use butter?

Joe: That's fattening!

Horsing Around

••

2 large baking potatoes, peeled

1 medium onion, peeled

1 egg, beaten

2 tablespoons all-purpose flour

1 teaspoon salt

¼ teaspoon ground white pepper

2 tablespoons vegetable oil

1. Grate the potatoes and onion into large shreds and combine them in a bowl. Stir in the egg, flour, salt, and white pepper. Blend well.

2. Heat the oil in a large skillet over medium–high heat for about 1 minute. Spoon the potato mixture into the skillet, forming 8 large cakes. Flatten the cakes with the back of a spatula. Cook them to brown the bottoms, about 3 minutes. Flip the cakes over and brown the other side for 3 minutes. Reduce the heat to low under the skillet. Continue to cook the cakes for 15 to 20 minutes longer, turning occasionally, until they are crisp on the outside and tender on the inside.

3. Serve with applesauce, if desired.

Makes 4 servings

Hassan Ben Sober's Hasty Hummus

Difficulty Level: Tadpole

Hassan Ben Sober should not have been so hasty.

Itching to steal the priceless King Rootin' Tootin' Diamond in *Malice in the Palace*, Ben Sober pays little mind to warnings by shifty partner Haffa Dalla that the diamond is cursed. Instead, he orders three restaurant waiters—the Stooges—to steal it for him.

Had he paused dispassionately for a moment, Ben Sober would have seen in the Stooges what the rest of us do every day: the cool calm and derring-do of international assassins. By enlisting Moe, Larry, and Shemp, he was practically giving the loot away.

Naturally, the Stooges succeed in stealing the Rootin' Tootin' Diamond. And the curse? The diamond's owner, the Emir of Shmow, is so terrified by the Stooges' Santa Claus disguises that he hasn't a moment to inflict one.

••

1 15½-ounce can chickpeas, drained

¼ cup tahini (sesame seed paste)

¼ cup fresh lemon juice

¼ cup olive oil

½ teaspoon garlic powder

½ teaspoon salt

1. Put the chickpeas into an electric blender or food processor. Add the remaining ingredients and blend until mixture is a smooth puree.

2. Spoon hummus into a small serving bowl. Serve with pita bread.

Makes 6 servings

Moe's Special Barbecue Sauce

Difficulty Level: Applebrain

At home, Moe was bravissimo at the barbecue, spectacular at the spit, a champion of the charcoal. Friends and family raved about his barbecued chicken and special sauce, and he and brother Shemp even dabbled with the idea of raising chickens professionally.

Moe flashed a glimpse of his potential at the barbecue in *Violent is the Word for Curly*, where he defrosts a frozen Curly by tying him to a gigantic rotisserie. "Twenty minutes to a pound," Moe declares. "We'll be here a month!"

Moe was so proud of his special barbecue sauce that he specifically mentions the tangy topper in a dilly of a story in his autobiography. Thankfully, Moe was generous with his recipes, and shared this one with Jean DeRita, wife of Curly Joe. Just remember to take it easy on the worshester-shister-sheer-sheer-shire-sire sauce. (I can't say *Worcestershire*!)

2 pints prepared barbecue sauce

6 tablespoons brown sugar

2 tablespoons Worcestershire sauce

½ cup molasses

½ cup corn syrup

Garlic powder

"Boy, I wish I had some worshester-shister-sheer-sheer-shire-sire sauce. I can't say Worcestershire!"

Moe, *Half-Wits Holiday*

1. Blend all ingredients in a medium bowl.

2. Stir well; store in refrigerator until ready to use.

Smells Like Somebody's Frying Onions!

Difficulty Level: Latherhead

A keen sense of smell is an essential part of every gourmet cook's repertoire. Get stuck with an ignorant bugle, and you'd best leave the cooking to Mama.

It is not always easy to tell whether your schnoz measures up. Simply claiming, as Moe does, that Limburger is your favorite fruit establishes little more than your fine taste in cheese sandwiches. Instead, you must subject yourself to a true olfactory test like the one Curly experiences in *Three Little Sew and Sews*.

While seducing a shapely young lady at a fancy dinner party, Curly carelessly sits on the burning cigar he had

These boots were made for fryin'.

misplaced moments earlier. Normal-nosed individuals in such a situation might simply have leaped from the sofa. But Curly, whose sense of smell approaches that of a bloodhound, remarks instead, "Smells like somebody's frying onions!" That is the measure of a natural born smeller.

Enjoy this recipe for the smell as much as for the taste; it is among the stinkiest in this cookbook.

Fried Onion Rings

••

1 egg

1 cup buttermilk

1 tablespoon vegetable oil

1 cup self-rising flour

1 extra-large sweet onion

Oil, for deep frying

Salt to taste

1. Combine the egg, buttermilk, and vegetable oil in a mixing bowl. Beat until well blended. Stir in the self-rising flour to form a smooth batter.

2. Cut off each end of the onion and peel it. Cut the onion into ¼-inch-thick slices and separate the slices into rings. Meanwhile, heat frying oil in a deep pan to 375°F.

3. Immerse the onion rings in the batter to coat them completely. Lift them out with a fork to let excess batter drip off, then drop them into the hot oil. Fry the rings until golden brown. Do not crowd the pan with too many rings at one time. Drain the fried rings on plain absorbent paper towels and sprinkle with salt. Serve hot.

Makes 3–4 servings

Maha's Aha? Not Blah Challah

Difficulty Level: Featherbrain

Today's schoolchildren pooh-pooh the need to learn a foreign language. English, they are convinced, is all they need.

Has none of them watched *Three Little Pirates*?

The Stooges never expect their vessel, *Garbage Scow 188*, to shipwreck off Dead Man's Island, and yet that is their sorry fate in *Three Little Pirates*. Worse, they are sentenced to death after Curly flirts with the ruler's fiancée. It would have been a sorry day for Stooge fans had Moe, Larry, and Curly been burned at the stake, but their lives are spared . . . all because Moe and Curly speak a foreign language.

Disguising themselves as wayfarers bearing wondrous gifts from mystical lands, they enchant the ruler of Dead Man's Island with their "Maha" routine, a mesmerizing exchange done in an exotic foreign dialect:

> "It's my favorite dish: biscuits! Biscuits all the time!"
>
> Curly, *Three Sappy People*

Moe: Maha?
Curly: A-ha?
Moe: You like to speak that?
Curly: I like to *talk* that!
Moe: Ras bañas ya-tee benafucci a timi nicaronja. That, how you say, that Pickle Puss, he askee taskee what dee chit vat syke you gottik?
Curly: Naathing!
Moe: Naathing?
Curly: Yooks!
Moe (translating): The Maharaja says he is the bearer of a rare jewel.

Naturally the ruler is overwhelmed by such exotic dialogue and immediately spares the lives of the gift-giving voyagers. (High school principals: you may wish to use this example to encourage students to enroll in foreign language courses.)

The recipe for Maha's Aha? Not Blah Challah recalls a day when quick thinking and an unusual foreign dialect saved three important lives. Prepare it lovingly and remember to add a sprinkle of ras bañas ya-tee benafucci to ensure safe passage.

The Maharaja, working up an appetite

••

1 16-ounce box hot roll mix

¾ cup hot water

4 tablespoons softened butter or margarine

2 eggs, beaten

1 egg yolk beaten with 1 tablespoon water

1. Preheat oven to 375°F. Grease a large baking sheet and set it aside.

2. Empty the contents of the box mix, including the yeast packet, into a large mixing bowl. Using an electric mixer with dough hooks on medium speed, beat in the hot water, butter, and 2 eggs. Mix 4 to 5 minutes to develop elasticity in the dough. Turn it out onto a floured surface to knead by hand 3 to 4 minutes, adding more flour as necessary to prevent dough from sticking. When the dough is very smooth, cover it with a large bowl for 5 minutes.

3. Push the dough out into a rectangle, 12 to 14 inches long, and divide into three long strands. Starting at one side of the loose ends, pinch them together. Braid the strands and seal the shape by pinching the opposite ends together. Transfer the braid to the baking sheet and cover the dough with a towel. Set aside to rise at room temperature for 45 minutes or until doubled in size. Uncover and brush dough with the yolk and water mixture.

4. Bake in the oven 25 to 30 minutes until deep golden brown. Cool the loaf on a wire rack.

Makes 8 servings

When in Rome . . .

Master the recipes in this book and word will spread quickly.

You'll be invited to attend high-society balls where fancy blue bloods will clamor to taste your specialties and raise a toast to your culinary craftsmanship. Rivers of champagne will flow in your honor, and wealthy socialites will compete for your affections.

But you must know how to behave amid such elegance; only an innocent would travel to such a soiree unprepared.

Luckily, the Stooges have been down this road. Follow their examples below, and you are certain to rise above the hoi polloi.

- Steal silver muglets, brass serving trays, and all loose silverware. Stash objects beneath your shirt and in the seat of your trousers in case a do-gooder acquaintance like Moe attempts to kick you in those regions.
- When dancing, dashingly swing your leg out far enough to kick the person dancing innocently beside you.
- If you have forgotten your formal wear, lure a well-dressed guest into the kitchen, then poke, punch, and pummel him until he surrenders his clothes.
- Add powdered alum to punch bowl for interesting puckering effect.
- Test fruit punch by tossing a glassful into a nearby flower-pot. If the flowers snap shut and die instantly, the punch is just right.
- When seated next to an attractive woman at the dinner table, reach underneath the table and lovingly grab her hand. After you realize that your friend had the same idea and that it is his hand you are holding, punish him by yanking out a tuft of hair from his arm.
- Greet elderly ladies by bowing and kissing their hands, being careful to bite off and swallow any large diamonds they might be wearing.
- For dramatic effect, handle ice cubes with a gigantic ice pick.
- Offer to refill the water glasses of guests by dragging a gas station style filling hose from the kitchen into the dining room.
- While eating, lift pinkies daintily to project a refined and cultured image.

Wild Hyacinth Rice

Difficulty Level: Egghead

The expert chef is careful not to allow strong fragrances to overtake his cooking.

Not because it ruins the food or displeases the diner. But because of what happens to Curly in *Grips, Grunts and Groans.*

Curly is a gentle soul, but a single whiff of Wild Hyacinth perfume is enough to turn him into a hurricane of punches, kicks, and devastating belly bops. Even world wrestling champ Ivan Bustoff can't hold a candle to Curly if there's a lovely lady in the crowd dabbing a drop of Wild Hyacinth.

That's the danger faced by the expert chef. Sometime, somewhere, a dinner guest will be as sensitive to the aroma of his cooking as Curly is to Wild Hyacinth. When that happens, innocent eaters can get hurt.

Wild Hyacinth Rice emits a heady aroma, so prepare it carefully. If no one at the table twitches, serve proudly. But if one of your guests begins to shuffle, shake, and cry, "Woo-woo-woo-woo!" replace recipe with bread and water. If symptoms continue, check your perfume; you just might be wearing Wild Hyacinth.

· ·

1 cup wild rice

½ cup slivered almonds

⅓ cup minced celery

¼ cup minced green onion

3 tablespoons butter or margarine

½ teaspoon dried thyme

3 cups canned chicken broth

1. Rinse the wild rice under cold water and set aside to drain.

2. Sauté the almonds, celery, and green onion in the butter in a medium saucepan over medium heat until the almonds begin to change color, about 5 minutes. Add the wild rice, thyme, and broth to the saucepan. Bring the liquid to a boil, cover the pan, and reduce the heat to low. Simmer wild rice until the liquid is absorbed and grains are tender and fluffy, 35 to 45 minutes. Serve immediately.

Makes 6 servings

Percy Pomeroy: Prisoner Number 41144's Honest Bread and Water

Difficulty Level: Jughead

The mission seems a cinch: If the Stooges recruit an honest man with executive ability, oil magnate B. O. Davis will pay them $5,000.

Invigorated by the challenge, Moe, Larry, and Curly break spontaneously into this peppy chant:

> *We're on our way for an honest man;*
> *We'll bring him back as fast as we can;*
> *Excelsior!*

The Stooges hit the streets but uncover nothing but a bunch of petty crooks. They do meet an honest dog, but it does not seem to possess enough executive ability.

Finally, the Stooges stumble across a weeping beauty who claims that her boyfriend, Percy Pomeroy, is the most honest man in the world. The only catch is that he's in prison, accused of a crime he did not commit.

Buoyed by their discovery, the Stooges bust into jail and immediately locate Pomeroy, prisoner number 41144. In a bold stroke of genius, Pomeroy and the Stooges paint bold strokes of paint over their prison grays until each appears to be wearing a guard's uniform. Escape seems certain until the men reach the prison gates; that's where the warden happens to be admitting a crook of a different stripe, B. O. Davis, aka Lone Wolf Louie, the country's biggest bond swindler. For the Stooges that means no $5,000, no escape, and no glory. Just a lifetime of honest bread and water.

•••

1 cup warm water

1 envelope active dry yeast

2 tablespoons sugar

2 tablespoons vegetable oil

1 teaspoon salt

3 cups flour

1. Place the warm water in a large mixing bowl and sprinkle with the yeast. Let soak 5 minutes. Add the sugar, oil, and salt; then begin adding the flour little by little. Beat into a stiff dough. Turn it out onto a floured surface and knead until it feels smooth and elastic, about 7 minutes. Place the dough into a large greased bowl, cover, and set aside to rise at room temperature for 1 hour or until doubled in size.

2. Punch the dough down and push it evenly into a greased 9" × 5" loaf pan. Cover the pan with a towel and let it rise a second time until the dough reaches the top of the pan, 30 to 45 minutes. Meanwhile, preheat an oven to 375°F.

3. Bake in the oven 35 to 40 minutes until deep golden brown. Remove the loaf from the pan to cool on a wire rack.

Makes 8 servings

> "I'd like to meet the guy who invented these barbed wire pineapples."
> Curly, on artichokes, in *Sock-A-Bye Baby*

N'yuk N'yuk N'Yams

Difficulty Level: Bonehead

If it's true that a man's laugh reveals his soul, Curly is the most soulful man in the world.

Whether working or playing, running from police or standing before a firing squad, Curly is certain to lighten the moment with a delightful "N'yuk n'yuk n'yuk." During earthquakes and gunfights, calamities and tragedies, Curly's n'yuks make catastrophes nice.

What better food to commemorate the irresistible exuberance of Curly's trademark n'yuks than the festive yam? Prepare this recipe precisely, and you may not be able to stop laughing yourself.

···

1 cup apple cider

½ cup honey

2 tablespoons fresh lemon juice

1½ tablespoons butter

2 medium–large yams or sweet potatoes, peeled

1. Combine the cider, honey, lemon juice, and butter in a medium saucepan. Bring the mixture to a simmer over medium–low heat and cook for 5 minutes.

2. Meanwhile, cut the yams into ¼- to ½-inch-thick slices. Add them to the cider mixture and cover the pan. Simmer until yams test fork-tender, about 30 minutes. Remove the slices with a slotted spoon and place them on a serving dish. Cover the dish to keep the yams warm.

3. Raise the heat under the saucepan to medium–high to reduce the cooking juices to a syrup consistency, about 10 minutes, or ½ cup in volume. Pour the hot syrup evenly over the yam slices and serve immediately.

Makes 4 servings

Chapter 2

Appetizers

"He's so goofy you could knock him down with a handful of peanuts—without the shells!"

Larry, *Fright Night*

This Fish Looks Like Moe!

Difficulty Level: Scrabblehead

Moe has a distinctive face. And a haircut that's unmistakable.

That's why it's difficult to fathom how the other Stooges so often fail to recognize him. Most of us recognize Moe the moment we see him.

In *Listen, Judge,* Larry and Shemp mistake Moe for a gopher and beat him senseless. In countless haunted mansions, the other Stooges confuse Moe for a ghoul or goblin and bludgeon him with a smorgasbord of deadly weapons.

But the most painful case of mistaken identity occurs while the Stooges are ice fishing in *Rockin' Thru the Rockies.* Elated by the violent tug at the end of their line, Larry and Curly fail to notice that the ornery fish they have reeled in looks familiar. Eager to kill the tremendous prize, Larry brains the fish with an iron rod until the truth finally dawns on Curly.

"This fish looks like Moe!" Curly exclaims.

Sadly for Larry and Curly, Moe is less sympathetic than the average fish.

There is no mistaking this recipe for anything but gefilte fish. Enjoy it in good health, but do not club it with an iron rod; you never really know who that fish might be.

No-Fuss Gefilte Fish

· ·

1 14½-ounce jar gefilte fish in jellied broth

¼ teaspoon sugar

½ small onion, sliced thin

½ celery stalk, sliced thick

1 medium carrot, sliced thick

Red horseradish, as needed

1. Empty the contents of the jar into a saucepan. Add the sugar, then add the sliced vegetables. Bring the mixture to a simmer, cover the pan, and cook over low heat until carrots are tender, 10 to 12 minutes.

2. Using a slotted spoon, remove the gefilte fish and the carrots to a bowl. Pour the hot broth through a strainer over the bowl. Discard the celery and onion. Let the gefilte fish mixture cool in the broth to room temperature.

3. Chill in the refrigerator, if desired. Serve the gefilte fish and carrots with some of the jellied broth and lots of red horseradish.

Makes 4 servings

Even away from the set, the Stooges were careful to ensure that everyone enjoyed his meal.

Dr. Howard! Dr. Fine! Dr. Howard! Three-Alarm Bean Dip

Difficulty Level: Oysterbrain

Debate still rages among medical professionals. Were the Stooges truly qualified to practice medicine?

Naysayers point out that the Stooges routinely leave surgical tools inside patients, administer anesthesia with a wooden mallet, and claim to have "graduated with the highest temperatures in our class."

Believers point to the Los Arms Hospital in the Stooge film *Men in Black.*

It is at Los Arms that interns Moe, Larry, and Curly prove willing to burst through glass doors, knock over wheelchair-bound patients, and terrorize nurses whenever the intercom box makes that clarion call, "Dr. Howard! Dr. Fine! Dr. Howard!" And it is at the Los Arms that the Stooges revolutionize interhospital travel by shuttling between corridors aboard bicycles, horses, and even miniature race cars.

Sadly, the Stooges forfeited much respect in the medical community after they used revolvers to shoot the hospital intercom to death. Physicians, it turns out, don't consider the annoying personality of an intercom as an excuse for murder.

Dr. Howard, Dr. Fine, and Dr. Howard should, however, be honored for the positives they brought to the field of medicine. This potent recipe for three-alarm bean dip will cause any chef to graduate with the highest temperature in his class.

••

1 15-ounce can pinto beans, rinsed and drained

¾ cup hot salsa or red jalapeño salsa

¼ cup sour cream

Hot sauce to taste

1. Put the beans into a mixing bowl and mash them with a handheld potato masher. Stir in the salsa and sour cream. Mix well. Add hot sauce to taste.

2. Serve with corn tortilla chips.

Makes 6–8 servings

> **Moe:** Now, Where is this John Smith?
>
> **Joe:** In his office, next door to a barbecue pit.
>
> **Larry:** Hey, do barbecues have pits?
>
> *Quiz Whizz*

A Modest Recipe from the Kitchen of Antonio Zucchini Salami Gorgonzola de Pizza

Difficulty Level: Knucklehead

The Stooges are hasty in *Tricky Dicks*.

Desperate to capture the killer of Slug McGurk, the three detectives pounce on suspicious-looking Antonio Zucchini Salami Gorgonzola de Pizza. And why not? An Italian organ grinder with a British accent doesn't just walk into a police station for nothing.

Detectives Moe, Larry, and Shemp grill de Pizza, but to no avail. De Pizza's monkey, however, takes to police work like a natural; when McGurk's actual killer bursts into the station, the sharpshooting primate saves de Pizza—and the Stooges—by dishing out justice the old-fashioned way: with a .38-caliber Smith & Wesson.

Had the Stooges not been so quick to point the finger at de Pizza, perhaps they might have coaxed an old-world recipe from the deliciously named organ grinder. Enjoy this better-late-than-never dish from the kitchen of Antonio Zucchini Salami Gorgonzola de Pizza. But please, out of respect for crime-fighting primates, do not add monkey.

···

1 10-ounce can refrigerated pizza crust dough

2 tablespoons pizza sauce

2 ounces thinly sliced pepperoni

½ cup shredded mozzarella cheese

1. Preheat oven to 425°F. Lightly grease a large cookie sheet.

2. Remove the rolled dough from the can. Push the dough into a strip about 16 inches long and 4 inches wide, and place it on the cookie sheet. Spread the sauce over the dough evenly. Cover sauce with a single layer of the pepperoni slices, overlapping them slightly. Sprinkle with cheese.

3. Bake the pizza strip in the oven 12 to 14 minutes, or until crust is golden brown and cheese has melted. Cut the strip into 8 slices and serve warm.

Makes 8 servings

Curly: Maybe he'd like a smarty-coke, a party smoke, an o-key-doke . . . this feathered apple.

Moe: Y'artichoke.

Curly: You, too!

Sock-A-Bye Baby

Cedric the Blacksmith's Ironclad Chopped Liver

Difficulty Level: Dumb Ox

Viewers rarely shed tears during a Three Stooges film. But even a lumberjack would whimper during *Squareheads of the Round Table*, in which an elitist king refuses to allow his daughter to marry her beau, Cedric the Blacksmith. (Even Shemp's logic—that thousands of women marry Smiths every year—does not persuade the king.)

Undeterred, Cedric enlists three royal troubadours—Moe, Larry, and Shemp—to sing a lovesick sonnet in three-part harmony outside the courtyard window of Princess Elaine. That song, sung lovingly out of tune, still breaks hearts today. (Sung to the classical strains of *Sextetrum Lucia*, with Elaine's part in parentheses):

> *Oh, Elaine, Elaine come out, babe;*
> *Take a look who's standing here, right here;*
> *The big boy is here, we see the coast is clear;*
> *He wants to see you, so come out on your front porch.*

> *Oh, Elaine, come out, oh, please come out;*
> *Time is short, the guards are hanging about;*
> *Your Cedric's here, no kiddin', Cedric's here.*

> *(I see, I see my darling Cedric standing there;*
> *I know, I know that I will soon be in his arms again.)*

> *She knows, she knows that she will soon be in his arms again!*

> *(Nee, but flee, the Black Prince is lurking near!*
> *I will raise the shade, the lovely shade, when the coast is clear.)*

Love prevails, as it always does, and the king consents to the wedding of Cedric and Elaine. No one knows what was served at the royal wedding reception, but given Cedric's occupation, it is virtually certain that he provided a food rich in iron, something romantic, something very much like Cedric the Blacksmith's Ironclad Chopped Liver.

• •

1½ cups water

8 ounces chicken livers

1 tablespoon rendered chicken fat

1 medium onion, chopped coarse

1 hard-cooked egg, shelled and chopped

Salt and freshly ground black pepper to taste

1. Bring the water to a boil in a medium skillet. Add the livers and simmer over medium heat until firm and cooked, about 5 minutes. Drain the livers and set aside to cool.

2. Wipe the skillet dry and set over medium–low heat. Add the chicken fat and the onion, and sauté until soft, about 7 to 10 minutes.

3. Chop the cooled livers and combine with the chopped egg in a bowl. Add the sautéed onions to the bowl. Stir with a wooden spoon, mashing the ingredients with the back of the spoon while stirring, until consistency is slightly pasty. Season with salt and pepper.

4. Serve chopped livers with crackers or melba toast.

Makes 4–6 servings

Woo-Woo-Woo-Woo Cheese Fondue

Difficulty Level: Laughing Hyena

Some claim it's a song. Others insist it's a war cry. But everyone agrees that Curly's "Woo-woo-woo-woo!" means excitement.

Curly emits a "Woo-woo-woo-woo!" when he's frightened, perturbed, stirred, struck, awed, agitated, enlightened, enraptured, and embalmed. He cries "Woo-woo-woo-woo!" when ready to fight, flee, spin, or wobble. Whatever the film, Stooge fans know to hold tight if they hear that trademark ululation "Woo-woo-woo-woo!"

Finally, there is a recipe that combines Curly's love for excitement with his love for cheese. You can prepare Woo-Woo-Woo-Woo Cheese Fondue in silence, but in the name of all that is thrilling about cooking, please exclaim "Woo-woo-woo-woo!" while preparing this dynamic and daring cheese fondue.

....

1¼ cups dry white wine

⅛ teaspoon garlic powder

1 pound shredded Swiss cheese

1 tablespoon cornstarch

⅛ teaspoon ground nutmeg

1 loaf (1 pound) French bread,
cut into 1½-inch chunks

1. In a 3-quart saucepan, combine 1 cup of the wine and the garlic powder. Bring to a simmer over low heat. Slowly stir in the cheese, letting some melt before adding more. Do not let mixture boil.

2. When all the cheese is melted, mix the cornstarch and nutmeg with the remaining ¼ cup wine in a dish. Add it to the cheese mixture, stirring until smooth and thick, about 5 minutes.

3. Transfer the fondue to a chafing dish set over a low flame.

Makes 4 servings

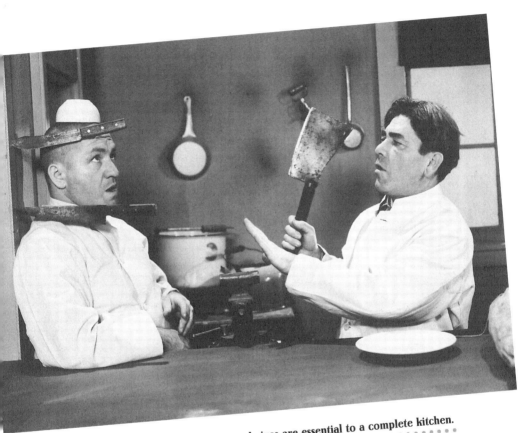

Sharp knives are essential to a complete kitchen.

Can o' Peas or Derves

Difficulty Level: Mental Midget

Party cooking is a strange business. Ruin the main course and guests will forgive. But mess up the hors d'oeuvres and famished guests will glare as if you'd kidnapped their firstborn.

The Stooges understand the importance of hors d'oeuvres and labor mightily to concoct some of history's most exquisite examples. None, however, is finer than Can o' Peas or Derves, an appetizer they whip up at the high-society gala celebrating the engagement of no-good Prince Shaam to unsuspecting heiress Mrs. Van Bustle in *Crash Goes the Hash*.

Normal chefs would swell with pride to possess such a recipe. But the fact that you own this cookbook proves there is nothing normal about you. Read the following dialogue carefully and you will come to know Can o' Peas or Derves intimately, as the masters did.

Butler (to Moe): Incidentally, are you good on stews?

Curly (interrupting): Soitenly! He's always half-stewed!

Butler: Now, whenever you're ready, serve the drinks and don't forget the canapés.

Moe: Canapés? Oh, you mean the toast with the lace curtains.

Butler: Such levity! You remind me of the Three Stooges.

Curly: Hey, that's an insult!

Butler (flustered): Well now, I was only joking. Carry on.

Curly: Now what would he want with a can of peas?

Moe: Not can of peas . . . canapés!

Larry: Not can of peas, canopies! One of us is crazy and it's not you.

Moe: Right! Canapés. Hors d'oeuvres.

Curly: Which one? Can o' peas or derves? Make up your mind!

Moe: You put 'em on crackers. They give you an appetite like a horse.

Curly: Oh, animal crackers!

Moe: Go on. Make the canapés . . .

Curly: With animal crackers!

Moe: Listen, featherbrain. Take this camera. Keep your eyes open. The minute you see the prince, snap his picture. Make it a candid picture.

Curly: Yeah, a candid picture of a can of peas!

Stooges' Can o' Peas or Derves

• •

1 can of peas

1 box Puppo Dog Biscuits

1 jar green olives

Arrange dog biscuits in distressingly sloppy fashion on a sterling silver serving tray. Dump peas randomly over dog biscuits, being careful to spill several peas onto a nearby priceless Persian rug. Place single olive on each biscuit for color and beauty. Serve to stuffy guests.

Dinner among friends.

• • • • • • • • • • • • • •

Another Can o' Peas or Derves: Bruschetta

....

1 medium tomato, cored

2 tablespoons finely chopped onion

1 garlic clove, chopped fine

1 tablespoon chopped fresh oregano or basil

½ tablespoon fresh lemon juice

Salt and freshly ground black pepper to taste

Country bread slices

Olive oil

1. Cut the tomato in half. Squeeze out the seeds and juice, and discard. Chop the tomato and put into a bowl. Add the onion and garlic, stirring to mix. Stir in the herb and lemon juice. Season with salt and pepper, and set aside.

2. Broil or toast bread slices, as needed, and brush one side with olive oil. Spoon the tomato topping onto the oiled side of the toast. Serve immediately.

Makes 4 servings

Hangemall Prison's Jailbreak Jubilee

Difficulty Level: Clumsy Ox

For more than twenty glorious years, there wasn't a prison in the world that could hold the Stooges. No steel bar was thick enough, no watchman savvy enough to stop these Houdinis of the jail cell.

History has long wondered how the Stooges—who most often were imprisoned after committing shocking mental blunders—could have fashioned such ingenious escapes.

The truth is that the Stooges did not act alone. Countless jailbreaks were pulled off by their accomplices—female accomplices.

Occasionally these shapely beauties would distract jailers who had a taste for blonds. More often these loyal ladies would prepare bountiful "last meals" consisting of wonderful breads, appetizers, entrees, and desserts. Soon thereafter, the Stooges would bust out. Wardens were baffled. Food fans knew those meals were bursting with iron.

Stooges' Hangemall Prison's Jailbreak Jubilee

1 very long French bread

1 vegetable pot pie

1 chubby chicken

1 thermos of hot soup

1 hammer

1 rusty file

1 snaggletooth saw

1 curvaceous girlfriend who is
inexplicably in love with you

Politely instruct girlfriend to cram hammer, rusty file, and snaggletooth saw into various foods, then deliver to you on death row. Selflessly offer guard your hot soup. Remove jailbreak tools from food. With each noisy slurp the guard takes, use tools to cut through prison bars until you find yourself gloriously free.

Another Jailbreak Jubilee: Rye Bread Dip

⅔ cup softened cream cheese

4 ounces (about ⅔ cup) corned beef slices,
shredded fine

½ cup Thousand Island dressing

1. Combine the cream cheese, shredded corned beef, and salad dressing in a bowl. Blend well.

2. Serve the dip with rye toast points, rye crackers, or rye bagel chips.

Makes 1½ cups dip, enough for 4–6 servings

Honest Icabod Slipp's Shady Subpoena Chip Dip

Difficulty Level: Picklebrain

Honest Icabod Slipp picked the wrong guys to swindle in *Hold That Lion!* and *Loose Loot.* Moe, Larry, and Shemp do not sit idly by while some crook bamboozles them out of an inheritance.

Armed with subpoenas and determined to lay their hands on the shady Slipp, Larry and Shemp break into this inspirational crime-fighting chant:

Larry:	We'll get that filthy lucre!
Shemp:	The moolah!
Larry:	The geedus!
Together:	No slippery guy named Slipp;
	Is ever gonna cheat us!
	A-zoop! A-zope! A-zoe!

At Slipp's office, however, each of the Stooges suffers a setback after being knocked unconscious by the lead-fisted crook. It is not the policy of this cookbook to celebrate criminals, but you've got to hand it to Slipp; he traveled light and fast, and this chip dip does the same. Prepare it honestly and with good intentions; you never know when three angry heirs might burst into your kitchen shouting, "A-zoop! A-zope! A-zoe!"

....

1 4⅜-ounce tin sardines, drained

3 tablespoons mayonnaise

3 tablespoons sour cream

2 tablespoons minced green onion

¼ teaspoon curry powder

¼ teaspoon lemon juice

⅛ teaspoon bottled hot sauce, or more to taste

1. Mash the sardines in a bowl with a fork. Add the mayonnaise, sour cream, and onion. Mix well. Stir in the curry powder, lemon juice, and hot sauce.

2. Serve the dip with potato chips.

Makes 3–4 servings

How Burly Is Curly?

● ● ● ● ● ● ● ● ● ● ● ● ● ●

202 pounds? 292? 302?

In *Punch Drunks*, Curly flirted with svelte, but in *Dizzy Pilots* he was positively roly-poly. No wonder it's so hard to guess his girth.

The subject of Curly's tonnage has weighed heavily on Stooge fans for ages. Thanks to *The Official Three Stooges Cookbook*, there's now a method to determine precisely where Curly tips the scales.

It comes from a formula invented by Moe. In *Violent is the Word for Curly*, Curly is accidentally frozen solid inside an ice truck. In a heroic effort to defrost the "frozen dainty," Moe ties Curly to a giant revolving barbecue spit and then builds a roaring fire beneath him. Poking his rotating pal's belly with a stick, Moe provides the magic formula.

"Twenty minutes to a pound," Moe declares. "We'll be here a month!"

Using Moe's set of precise figures, Curly's weight can be determined thusly:

1 month = 30 days = 720 hours = 43,200 minutes

20 minutes/pound = 2,160 pounds

Curly, therefore, weighs 2,160 pounds.

Thus ends the debate.

Jimmy's Not-So-Gentle Baby Food

Difficulty Level: DO NOT ATTEMPT

The Stooges love kids, and that's never more evident than when they take in Jimmy, a baby abandoned on their doorstep in *Sock-A-Bye Baby*.

But just because the Stooges are masters of adult cooking does not mean they understand the intricacies of baby food.

This recipe, which Moe lovingly prepared for Jimmy, is for educational purposes only. (Moe's intentions were pure, but baby food should probably *never* contain herring.)

....

1 dash Worcestershire sauce

1 squirt onion juice

6 ⅞ ounces Limburger cheese
(taken from a dusty mousetrap)

1 cup flour

2 stalks celery

4 radishes

1 artichoke

1 jar herring

1 box bicarbonate of soda

Combine all ingredients except flour in mixing bowl. Have meddlesome friend sneeze into flour, covering your face in pasty white. Poke friend's eyes.

Before serving, sing Curly's dramatic trademark song, "I Was Born in Brazil":

> *I was born in Brazil and I grew on a tree;*
> *When they shook the tree then I fell down;*
> *Then they put me in a bag;*
> *And they fastened on a tag;*
> *And they shipped me off to New York town.*

Chapter 3

"Here y'are, folks. Get your ice-cold lemonade! It's delicious, you'll love it!"

Curly, serving lemonade to blue-blooded guests at a high-society party in *Crash Goes the Hash*

Beverages

Shaved Ice

Difficulty Level: Imbecile

Ordinary cooks take ice for granted simply because it contains only one ingredient.

Not Chef Curly.

Rather than bludgeon a block of ice into humdrum cubes, Chef Curly lovingly shaves his ice so that party guests might enjoy a more regal cooling experience with their beverages. Impatient waiters like Moe find little time for such indulgence, but that's probably because they do not observe the care Curly paid to one particular block of ice in *An Ache in Every Stake.*

....

1 big block of ice (about the size of a microwave)

1 towel

1 jar shaving cream

1 straightedge razor

1 razor strap

1 chair (preferably with a high seat)

Place block of ice on chair. Fasten towel around block of ice. Sharpen straightedge razor on strap. Politely say to ice, "You're new in the neighborhood, aren't you? Once over lightly, yes sir!" Pluck a hair from your head and test sharpness of razor by cutting the hair. Ask ice if it would like a hot towel. Vigorously spread shaving cream across the face of the ice. Strike up this conversation with the ice: "Tell me, is it as warm in the summer as it is in the country, or vice versa? Are you married or happy? You have a very tough beard, like nails!" Wipe shaving cream off ice and place stubble into your pockets. Remark to ice, "Pardon me, did you have a pink tie on? No? Well, here's your lip."

Toasting the Light Fantastic

● ● ● ● ● ● ● ● ● ● ● ●

Drinking is a lost art, a gentleman's sport that has devolved into crude gulping and swallowing. Gone are the days when men made heartfelt toasts, slapped each other on the back and imbibed fine spirits to celebrate the good life.

The Stooges savor drinking, and their trademark toasts reveal them to be men of the world. Try some for yourself and discover what it's like to enjoy the life of a liquor connoisseur.

"A couple a pip pips, a little barbecue, and what have you!"
Debonair aside made over scotch by detective Shemp to a devious blond in *Who Done It?* and *For Crimin' Out Loud.* She tries to murder him anyway.

"And the rest of the day for myself!"
Suave toast from gentleman Shemp after Moe salutes him by exclaiming, "Top o' the morning to you" in *Fuelin' Around* and *Hot Stuff.*

"Here's eggs in your vest!"
Curly in *Crash Goes the Hash*

"Ver G'harget!" "Over the River!" and "Skip the Gutter!"
Trio of exhuberant toasts offered by the Stooges to a drugstore customer who has ordered a swig of moonshine in *Pardon My Scotch.* Had the customer spoken Yiddish, he might have been less inclined to drink; "Ver G'harget" means "drop dead."

"I know how!"
Shemp's triumphant counter-toast in *Gypped in the Penthouse* after Larry proposes, "Here's how."

"Down the hatchet! Hooray!"
Glorious salutes offered by Moe and Shemp in *The Ghost Talks* and *Creeps* as the Stooges prepare to drink a bottle of milk with Sir Tom, a long-dead spirit imprisoned in a suit of armor.

Moe's Nerve Tonic

Difficulty Level: Ignoramus

Woe is Moe.

Years of poking, slapping, and gouging—plus the intense pressure of being the brains of the outfit—finally catch up with him in *Idiots Deluxe*, in which he suffers a nervous breakdown.

His doctor prescribes peace and quiet. Those close to him are less sensitive to his plight.

A rude mouse in Moe's apartment, for example, has the nerve to scamper across the carpet, forcing Moe to scold the tiny critter by screaming, "Quit stomping around!"

Less forgivable are roommates Larry and Curly, who begin practicing their "Original Two-Man Quartet" musical act complete with drum, trombone, and crashing cymbals. The cacophony is enough to split Moe's skull—especially when Curly's trombone slide flies away from his instrument and wraps itself around Moe's neck.

Thank goodness for modern medicine. Were it not for Moe's constant ingestion of prescription nerve tonic and vitamins A.P.U., he might never have survived to continue punching, pinching, poking, and maintaining order.

Patients with frazzled nerves have long yearned for the secret formula to Moe's nerve tonic. They need twitch no longer. Here, in the interest of a calmer world, is that peaceful recipe.

Moe: Listen, Bustoff, you can't drink that; that's alcohol!

Bustoff: "Noooo, that's not alcohol. That's just a little tequila, vodka, and cognac.

Curly: Oh, that's different. Go ahead!

Grips, Grunts and Groans

Stooges' Moe's Nerve Tonic

••

1 jumbo bottle vitamins A.P.U.
(must be type made by Shtunk Mfg. Co.)

1 jigger of sastrophonia

2 cups anacanapanasan

1 handful 200 percent wool
(taken from a sheep who led a double life)

Pour jigger of sastrophonia into metal tumbler. Add anacana-panasan until mixture billows white smoke. Sprinkle vitamins A.P.U. into potion until projectiles are hurled from tumbler, making fearsome missile sounds. Garnish with handful of 200 percent wool. Ingest tumbler, being careful to make constant gulping sound until every drop is consumed. Relax.

The Original Two-Man Quartet is not in tune with Moe's nerves.

Another Moe's Nerve Tonic: Cranberry Juice Drink

··

²⁄₃ cup cranberry juice cocktail

⅓ cup tonic water

⅛ lime, cut into a wedge

Ice cubes

Pour the cranberry juice cocktail into a highball glass. Add the tonic water and squeeze the lime wedge into the drink. Fill the glass with ice cubes and stir well.

Makes 1 serving

Breath O' Heather Vat 106 Plus

Difficulty Level: Applehead

> "With a little luck, it should get to be 250."
>
> Moe, after tasting a rare scotch its owner claims to be aged 150 years in *Hot Scots*

Want to impress your favorite scotch connoisseur? Tell 'em you've tried Breath O' Heather Vat 106 Plus.

Of course, this technically won't be accurate. The true inventors of Breath O' Heather— Scottish distillers McSniff (Larry), McSnort (Curly), and McSnuff (Moe)—never revealed the recipe. But a close inspection of their methods in *Pardon My Scotch* allows the savvy imbiber to deduce the fundamentals.

Not all tasters agree on its quality, but the potency of Breath O' Heather is questioned by none. Not since prohibition was repealed has scotch tasted this . . . Scottish.

Breath O' Heather Rob Roy

....

5 ice cubes

2½ ounces blended scotch whisky

½ ounce dry vermouth

1 twist of lemon peel

Put 2 of the ice cubes into a cocktail shaker. Add the scotch and the dry vermouth. Stir it up well, then strain the liquid into a rocks glass. Add the remaining ice cubes and the twist of lemon peel.

Makes 1 serving

Nip and Tuck

Difficulty Level: Dumbbell

Fiery Confederate officer Colonel Buttz is a formidable military man. But he's met his match in Major Hyde (Curly) when it comes to drinking in *Uncivil Warriors*.

The Colonel is quite curious to sample a Nip and Tuck, Curly's drink of choice, but can't quite figure out what it is.

"One nip," Curly explains, "and they tuck you away for the night!"

....

¾ cup dry red wine

½ tablespoon sugar

⅛ teaspoon ground cloves

1 cinnamon stick

Combine the wine, sugar, and cloves in a small saucepan over medium heat. Slowly bring the mixture to a boil. Pour it into a mug and stir with the cinnamon stick.

Makes 1 serving

Eenar Fraapini

Difficulty Level: Hot Airedale

Physicians have long complained that Moe does not respect human eyes, hair, noses, or stomachs. Moe, they say, is a menace to the body.

None of these physicians ever saw *Up in Daisy's Penthouse.*
With Shemp collapsing from wedding day nerves, Moe might have been forgiven for pulling his friend's hair or gouging his eyes. Moe, however, takes his inspiration from Hippocrates and prescribes a medicinal cure.

> "Well, Doc, every time I squeeze my Adam's apple I can taste cider."
> Curly, *Nutty But Nice*

The Eenar Fraapini.
More potent than penicillin and tastier than tequila, the Eenar Fraapini is an original Moe concoction that ambivalent grooms still covet. Providing a burst of courage during a groom's most tentative moments, it is the only drink prospective brides are likely to endorse on their wedding day.

Stooges' Eenar Fraapini

1 bottle Bretta

2 jiggers Croomithistle

6 7/8 oz. Papeeptoomin

1 quart pickle juice

Mix ingredients, then shake until you become disoriented. Force upon ambivalent grooms and anyone else requiring a sudden burst of courage.

Another Eenar Fraapini: Frappé

....

1½ ounces brandy

1 ounce peppermint schnapps

½ cup crushed ice

Combine the brandy and schnapps in a measuring cup and stir to mix. Mound the crushed ice in a martini glass. Pour the brandy mixture over the ice.

Makes 1 serving

The finest butlers use only the finest tools.

Cut Throat Drug Store's Fountain of Youth

Difficulty Level: Head-Clunker

What men crave and Ponce de León missed, the Stooges discover in *All Gummed Up* and *Bubble Trouble*.

The fountain of youth.

It isn't easy. The rubber boot the Stooges use to mix their potion at their Cut Throat Drug Store looks ready to dissolve. And Shemp is uncooperative, applying duct tape to his mouth and covering his face with a fencer's mask to avoid sampling early versions of the formula.

Despite setbacks (Shemp mistakenly adds jumbo Mexican jumping beans and turns jumpy, not younger), the Stooges persevere, adding subtle ingredients like zendayfus, mishegas, pyareecon, and cotton until the formula is just right. After geriatric prune Mrs. Flint gulps a dose and is transformed into a shapely blond, the Stooges know they've discovered a gold mine.

Prepare this recipe with caution. Drink too much and you, too, might turn out like old Amos Flint, who gulped so much of the Stooges' formula that he bypassed youth and turned into a tiny infant.

Stooges' Cut Throat Drug Store's Fountain of Youth

• •

1 jigger of zendayfus

2 squirts of mishegas

3 pints of pyareecon

4 balls cotton

Dash each of eenginzoemen and anacanapanasan

2 cups jumbo Mexican jumping beans

1 used fisherman's boot (knee-length)

**On the verge of miraculous discovery: a bit more eenginzoemen
and the Stooges will perfect the fountain of youth!**

Contemplate how rich the fountain of youth will make you.
Excitedly mix zendayfus, mishegas, pyareecon, and cotton into
fisherman's boot. Shake violently until mixture smokes and whis-
tles. Add jumbo Mexican jumping beans, then sample for effect.
Begin jumping uncontrollably until a friend or loved one holds
you down.

Adjust recipe by adding eenginzoemen and anacanapanasan.
Summon an old person who doesn't have much to lose and ask
that person to sample formula. If it's too strong, that person will
turn into an infant. Adjust potency until the elderly become
young and beautiful.

Another Fountain of Youth Invigorating Drink

....

⅔ cup reduced-sodium Bloody Mary mix or
tomato juice

⅓ cup sauerkraut juice, drained from sauerkraut

¼ teaspoon finely crushed caraway seeds

Ice cubes

Jigger of vodka (optional)

Combine the Bloody Mary mix and sauerkraut juice in a highball glass. Stir in the crushed caraway seeds. (If you're using the
tomato juice option, lemon juice and horseradish may be added
to taste.) Add ice cubes to fill the glass. Stir in vodka, if desired.

Makes 1 serving

Moe's Punch

Difficulty Level: Chucklehead

Where would Moe be without his punch?

The punch is the cornerstone of Moe's disciplinary arsenal.
Used at close range, it knocks wise guys cold and persuades
strangers to see things Moe's way.

Moe's stomach punch is especially devastating. Technical
types insist that a kettledrum is used to make the booming
sound whenever Moe punches, but a glance at the unhappy face of the recipient is enough to convince anyone that Moe's punch is the real deal.

"A toochy froochy!"

Curly's term for fruit punch
in *An Ache in Every Stake*

Moe's punch also is a team player, working tirelessly to complement his dazzling array of pokes, pinches, and pulls. Larry, especially, would love to strike back after an eye poke from Moe. The reason he refrains? Moe's punch.

This invigorating recipe for Moe's Punch will pick you right up . . . and lay you right down, too. Prepare it sparingly and drink only when you need to straighten things out the old-fashioned way, the Moe way, with a good old-fashioned punch.

• •

2 cups tropical fruit juice blend
(100 percent juice), chilled

½ cup fresh orange juice

2 tablespoons fresh lime juice

½ cup ginger ale, chilled

Ice cubes

1. In a small pitcher, combine the fruit juice blend with the orange and lime juices. Store in the refrigerator until ready to serve.

2. Stir in the ginger ale and pour into punch glasses. Add ice cubes to each glass before serving.

Makes 4 servings

> **"The rum went through this punch on stilts!"**
> Curly, commenting on the weakness
> of the fruit punch at a party in
> *Three Sappy People*

K. O. Bossy's Carrot County Chocolate Milk

Difficulty Level: Wise Guy

Chocolate milk is a staple of any gourmet meal. So why do most chefs insist on buying their chocolate milk from the grocery store?

Authentic chocolate milk comes only from the cow. Watch K. O. Bossy (Curly) in *Busy Buddies*. He knows how to get milk directly from the source.

Stooges' K. O. Bossy's Carrot County Chocolate Milk

1 cow costume

1 jumbo bottle of milk

1 rubber glove

Enter a nearby cow-milking contest. Recruit two pals to climb inside the cow costume; then lead that cow into the boxing ring where the contest is held. Nickname yourself K. O. Bossy.

Listen to the referee's instructions carefully: "Now you know the rules. This contest goes four rounds and the guy who gets the most milk is the winner. Now shake hands and come out milking!"

Give your pals the jumbo bottle of milk and attach rubber glove to the top. Instruct pals to turn bottle over and pour milk out a slit in the bottom of the cow costume. Yank on the fingers of the rubber glove in order to "milk" the cow.

When the glove bursts off and milk floods into your pail, act surprised, and declare, like Curly, "Oh, sabotoogee!"

There's nothing like a stiff drink of milk among men.

Another Chocolate Milk

1 cup milk, cold or hot

2 tablespoons chocolate syrup

¼ teaspoon vanilla extract (optional)

Pour the milk into a drinking glass or cup. Add the syrup. Stir well to blend. Stir in the vanilla, if desired.

Makes 1 drink

The Art of (Seltzer Bottle) War

By purchasing this cookbook, you have assumed a risk.

The recipes contained inside are so delicious that some hungry scoundrel will surely try to snatch your snacks or apprehend your appetizers.

Don't be defenseless. Protect your cooking the Stooge way.

Use the seltzer bottle.

More shocking than the rolling pin and more forceful than the fork, the seltzer bottle is the weapon of choice whenever the Stooges get near food. Hardened criminals and veteran partygoers have been washed away by blasts from the Stooges' seltzer bottles, and it is the rare rascal who can outduel Moe, widely considered to be the fastest seltzer slinger in the history of motion pictures.

Only recently, since the advent of slow-motion video recorders, has man been capable of studying the subtle moves used by the Stooges in waging seltzer bottle warfare. Study these tips carefully and always keep a fully charged bottle nearby; you never know who might be lurking around that refrigerator door.

Winning the Seltzer Bottle War

1. Always aim seltzer bottle the wrong way, so that you absorb the first shocking blast yourself. Military strategists disagree with this recommendation, but it seems to snap the Stooges into a heightened state of agitation that is deadly for their enemies.

2. Aim for the mouth, and don't stop shooting. Disregard all enemy gurgling sounds and keep blasting.

3. If the seltzer bottle fizzles out, aim directly into your eye and pull trigger to inspect. Yes, this is risky, but is there any other way to test malfunctioning equipment?

4. When the seltzer bottle goes empty, run. The Stooges were masters of escape, and you should be, too.

Remember, a good chef is an armed chef. Use your seltzer bottle responsibly.

Mickey Finn

Difficulty Level: Petty Larceny Stooge

Luck rarely plays a part when the Stooges triumph over villains. Most often, brains, brawn, and determination do the trick.

But in *Pals and Gals*, the Stooges lean heavily on Dame Fortune, whose smile is the only thing between Shemp and six slugs from a .44.

Embroiled in a crooked card game with dirty-dealing bandit Doc Barker, Shemp's only hope for escape is the knockout drink being prepared for him behind the bar by Moe and Larry.

> **Shemp (holding a wine bottle):** You know, there's a thousand reasons why I shouldn't drink.
>
> **Moe:** No kiddin'?
>
> **Shemp:** Yep. A thousand reasons. But I can't think of one right now.
>
> *Baby Sitters Jitters*

"What do you know about mixing drinks?" Moe asks Larry. "Nothing," Larry replies. "That's fine!" exclaims Moe, and the two begin mixing the lethal brew. Moe is careful to pour Shemp a harmless sarsaparilla. But on the way to the card table, Moe gets jostled; now all the drinks look the same!

The gravity of the situation is not lost on Shemp. When one of Barker's gang proposes a toast by exclaiming, "Here's to a short life and a merry one," an ashen Shemp concedes, "Yeah, a very short life."

That's when luck intervenes. The Mickey Finns somehow find their marks, leaving Barker gasping for oxygen and Shemp healthy as a horse. But don't rely on such luck when mixing this recipe. Mark the Mickey Finns clearly and please, go easy on the paint.

Stooges' Mickey Finn

1 bottle Old Homicide (distilled Monday)

Molasses

Tabasco sauce

Seltzer

Eggs

Paint (any color)

Paint remover

1 black rubber boot (knee-length)

Mix Old Homicide, molasses, and Tabasco in rubber boot. Test seltzer bottle by squirting in friend's face; then add seltzer to boot.

Lift two eggs in the air, then express gleefully, "This oughta make 'em cackle!" Break eggs on friend's forehead, allowing yokes to drip into rubber boot. Accidentally add paint, but remedy situation by pouring in liberal amounts of paint remover.

Shake boot violently. (Friend may tickle you to facilitate shaking.) When mixture begins boiling and smoking, the proper strength has been achieved. Do not serve in paper cups or spill onto wood furniture.

> "It's a little heavy on the angora bitters. In fact, I think the goat walked right through it, I'm sure!"
>
> Moe, trying to politely describe the fruit punch that Curly has spiked with alum powder in *No Census, No Feeling*

> **Moe (mixing powerful drink):** This oughta pick him up.
> **Curly:** And lay him down, too!
>
> *Pardon My Scotch*

Another Mickey Finn

....

3 ounces vodka

¼ teaspoon pickled jalapeño juice
(from a jar of jalapeño slices)

Ice cubes

2 pickled jalapeño slices

1 cocktail onion

1. Pour the vodka into a rocks glass. Stir in the jalapeño juice and fill the glass with ice.

2. Spear the jalapeño slices and cocktail onion with a toothpick to garnish the drink.

Makes 1 serving

Chapter 4

Larry: Wait'll you see what we got for breakfast this morning!

Moe: Nice cold hotcakes smothered in vinegar!

Flagpole Jitters

Breakfast

Burned Toast and a Rotten Egg

Difficulty Level: Sawdusthead

The Stooges have little trouble dealing with enemies. A quick eye poke, face slap, or double stomach bomp, and most foes flee in terror.

But Moe, Larry, and Curly each battle a trickier trouble-maker: the tapeworm. This internal enemy might have driven men of average intelligence insane, but the Stooges know just how to defeat the pesty parasite, which often sets up shop in their stomachs: At restaurants, they order burned toast and a rotten egg.

Why burned toast and a rotten egg?

As Moe says, "I've got a tapeworm and it's good enough for him."

Stooges' Burned Toast and a Rotten Egg

....

1 smart-aleck chicken

1 metal ramp (6 feet long)

1 supercharged stove

Place chicken on a perch near the ceiling. Position metal ramp between the chicken and your countertop. Order the chicken to lay four hard-boiled eggs. As each egg trickles down the ramp, test by bouncing it off the ground. When eggs break instead of bouncing, shake fist and loudly threaten, "One more trick like that and you'll wind up southern fried!"

Scoop up eggs and shells and deposit in frying pan. Light stove, stand back, and allow stove to explode. When mixture covers the face of a short-tempered friend, ask, "Where are you going—to a Halloween party?"

The toast is done, but is it sufficiently burned?

Another Burned Toast and a Rotten Egg:
Scrambled Eggs with Toast

....

8 eggs, beaten

¼ cup sour cream

2 tablespoons butter or margarine

Salt, freshly ground black pepper to taste

4 slices of bread

Softened butter, for toast

1. Combine the eggs and sour cream in a bowl and beat with a fork until smoothly blended. Heat 2 tablespoons butter in a medium skillet over medium–high heat until melted.

2. Add the beaten eggs. Using a wide wooden spatula, push the eggs from one side of the pan to the other to stir them up. In about 2 minutes, the eggs will set softly into large curds. Remove skillet from the heat, season the eggs with salt and pepper, and cover the pan to keep the eggs warm.

3. Toast the bread slices and spread them with soft butter. Cut each toast slice in half to serve with the scrambled eggs.

Makes 4 servings

Flipper's Fluffy Ferblongent Flapjacks

Difficulty Level: Dumb Cluck

Among a Stooge fan's greatest regrets is that he will never taste Larry's cooking.

Larry had a special relationship with food. He insisted on cleanliness, and was known to use oversized meat cleavers to chase squealing dogs and cats from his kitchen. (This did not always please restaurant customers, but you never saw the board of health complain.)

No one spooled spaghetti like Larry. It is he, in *Love at First Bite*, who ingeniously winds a mile-long strand of spaghetti around a fork until the entire bowlful is wrapped around the utensil.

But Larry's greatest culinary achievement is his surefire recipe for pancakes. Begun innocently from a box of Mrs. Flipper's Fluffy Pancake Mix in *Rusty Romeos*, Larry makes esoteric interpretations of the instructions on the box until he produces triangular, rectangular, and square pancakes. Even Moe is bewildered by the strange-looking breakfast, and queries, "Hey, what is this, Phi Sigma Delta?"

"No," Larry says. "They're Flipper's Fluffy Ferblongent Flapjacks!" to which Moe replies, "Oh, a new sorority!" Had Moe been up on his Yiddish, he would have known that *ferblongent* means "extremely confused," and would certainly have forgiven such crazy shapes.

> "I admit the pancakes ain't so good, but the syrup is delicious!"
> Curly, after serving Moe pancakes with glue instead of maple syrup in *Healthy, Wealthy and Dumb*

Stooges' Flipper's Fluffy Ferblongent Flapjacks

1 box Mrs. Flipper's Fluffy Pancake Mix

2 eggs

1 can condensed milk

1 squeeze bag

1 bottle maple syrup

1 bottle Stix-Fast Glue

Though you need only 2 cups of Mrs. Flipper's Fluffy Pancake Mix, dump entire box into mixing bowl. Add two eggs (whole, with shells) and condensed milk (still in the can). Become horrified at the error of putting a tin can inside the bowl and remove it. Unwrap and discard the paper label; then replace tin can in bowl.

Being a great chef is a heavy burden.

Scoop mixture into squeeze bag; then squeeze odd shapes onto baking pan. Bake for 2 minutes at 950°F. Remove.

Pour Stix-Fast Glue into a bottle that appears identical to the bottle of maple syrup. Mistakenly place glue instead of syrup on breakfast table. Serve pancakes.

Another Flipper's Fluffy Ferblongent Flapjacks: Blueberry Pecan Pancakes

···

3½ cups pancake batter (made from a box mix
or see recipe on page 71)

1 cup fresh or frozen blueberries

½ cup coarsely chopped pecans, lightly toasted

1 teaspoon vegetable oil

1. Add the blueberries and the toasted pecans to the prepared pancake batter. Stir well to blend. Pour the batter into a pitcher.

2. Heat a lightly greased griddle or large skillet over medium heat. Pour out batter to form 5-inch circles, leaving 1 inch of space between. Cook until bubbles break the surface and open up into holes, then flip the cakes over and cook the other side until golden brown.

3. Transfer cooked pancakes to a platter. Place them in a warm oven while cooking the remaining cakes.

4. Serve pancakes warm with blueberry flavored syrup.

Makes 4 servings

Collision Mats

Difficulty Level: McNothing

"Are you casting asparagus on my cooking?"
With these bold words, Chef Curly defends the honor of pancake makers everywhere.

As a highly trained cook in *Busy Buddies*, he will not stand for a rude customer's remark that his pancakes "must be made out of reclaimed rubber." To prove it, he eats the hotcakes himself. Unfortunately, he soon coughs up enough feathers to stuff a quilt.

Something went wrong with Curly's pancakes (he calls them collision mats), but that small detail has been corrected here.

Stooges' Collision Mats

••

1 premixed bowl of pancake batter

1 squeeze bag with defective spout

1 industrial-size pants press

1 jumbo pair rusty scissors

Pour pancake batter into squeeze bag. Try to squirt batter into pan, but discover that the spout is clogged. While continuing to squeeze bag, look directly into spout to investigate the problem. Discharge batter into your face, eyes, and hair. Squeal in frustration.

Squeeze four balls of batter onto steaming pants press. Close press for 30 seconds and then open. Pancakes should be golden brown. Declare, "Oh, boy!" Lift pancakes with fork and then cut each pancake into three pieces with scissors. Stack pancakes on table and use for poker chips during afternoon card game.

Another Collision Mats: Traditional Buttermilk Pancakes

1½ cups all-purpose flour

1½ tablespoons sugar

2 teaspoons baking powder

½ teaspoon salt

2 large eggs

1½ cups buttermilk

¼ cup (½ stick) butter or margarine, melted

1 teaspoon vegetable oil

1. Combine the flour, sugar, baking powder, and salt in a bowl. Stir to mix, and set aside. In another bowl, beat the eggs with the buttermilk and the melted butter until well blended. Stir in the flour mixture, blending into a thick batter. Pour the batter into a pitcher.

2. Heat a griddle or large skillet over medium heat. Lightly grease the pan, and when hot, pour out batter to form 5-inch circles, leaving 1 inch of space between each one. Cook until bubbles break the surface and open up into holes and then flip the cakes over to cook the other side until golden brown.

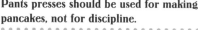

Pants presses should be used for making pancakes, not for discipline.

3. Transfer cooked pancakes to a platter. Hold them in a warm oven while cooking the remaining cakes.

4. Serve pancakes warm with maple syrup.

Makes 4 servings

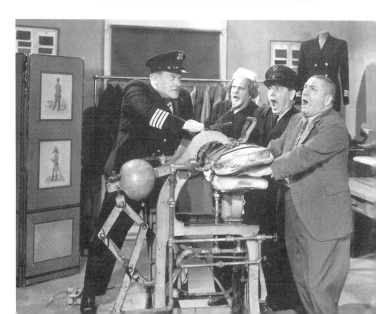

Eggs Sunny-Side Down and Don't Turn 'Em Over

Difficulty Level: Two-Ounce Brain

> **Moe:** We get a half a slice of ham and a half an egg apiece; you get a whole bone and a whole egg shell, and you're squawking!
>
> **Curly:** I'm sorry, Moe. Gee, you fellas are swell to me.
>
> *I Can Hardly Wait*

Some people consider Moe a pessimist for ordering his eggs sunny-side down in *Idiots Deluxe*. Others wonder why he refuses to turn them over.

But egg experts call him a genius.

Eggs prepared sunny-side down—especially when they are not turned over—have properties ordinary eggs lack. For example, they may be prepared in gallons of lard and can stick to walls and ceilings when flipped carelessly from the frying pan.

But don't take Moe's word for it. Prepare your own batch of Eggs Sunny-Side Down. And remember: absolutely, positively, don't turn 'em over.

Stooges' Eggs Sunny-Side Down and Don't Turn 'Em Over

4 eggs

1 tub of lard

1 oversized frying pan

1 pair jumbo rusty scissors

1 coffee grinder

1 dangerous stove

Hold eggs over coffee grinder. Use jumbo rusty scissors to cut each egg in half, allowing yoke and shells to fall into grinder.

Crank coffee grinder for 15 seconds while humming a delightful tune. Remove bottom tray full of egg and shell mixture.

Pour egg and shell mixture into oversized frying pan. Add three heaping shovelfuls of lard.

Turn dangerous stove to the high setting. When it fails to light, strike a match and light the burner yourself. Stand back and watch the stove explode into the air with a deafening bang.

Place frying pan onto burner, then vigorously shake the pan while the eggs cook. Continue to shake until a bossy friend like Moe comes into the kitchen and kicks you in the behind. Become startled and flip the pan backwards in a panic. When the eggs cover the eyes of your friend like a burglar's mask, raise your arms and surrender to the thief.

Never use too much of a good ingredient.

Another Eggs Sunny-Side Down and Don't Turn 'Em Over: Mushroom and Cheese Omelette

••

2 large mushroom caps, cleaned and sliced thin

1 tablespoon butter

Salt and freshly ground black pepper to taste

2 eggs, beaten

¼ cup shredded cheddar-jack cheese

1. In a 7-inch skillet over medium heat, cook the sliced mushrooms in ½ tablespoon of the butter until soft, 4 to 5 minutes. Season with salt and pepper. Remove the mushrooms from the skillet and set them aside.

2. Add the remaining ½ tablespoon butter to the skillet over medium–low heat. When the butter is melted, add the beaten eggs. Stir the eggs until lightly scrambled and softly set. Flatten eggs evenly with a spatula and spread with the cooked mushrooms. Sprinkle with the cheese. Slide a spatula under one side of the eggs and flip over to fold in half and cover the filling. Turn the omelette out onto a plate to serve.

Makes 1 serving

"Vitamins ABCDEF *Gee* I like food!"
Curly, after spotting a bountiful
buffet in *Matri-Phony*

Southern Comforter

Difficulty Level: Grapehead

Stooge fans do not associate Moe with a sensitive palate. In fact, Stooge fans associate Moe with very little that is sensitive. But in *Uncivil Warriors* he demonstrates a sophistication of the taste buds that is the envy of food connoisseurs.

When Judith, the enchanting daughter of Confederate Colonel Buttz, unwittingly bakes a cake containing more feathers than flour, she graciously informs the Stooges that the recipe is known as Southern Comfort. Always the gentleman, Moe chokes back the feathers, uses all his might to continue chewing, and replies politely, "Tastes more like Southern Comforter!"

· ·

8 slices day-old challah (or egg bread)

2 cups 2% milk

¼ cup (½ stick) butter, melted

1 teaspoon salt

½ teaspoon pepper

6 well-beaten eggs

16-ounce package shredded cheddar cheese

1. Cube the bread and set it aside.

2. Combine the milk, butter, salt, pepper, and eggs. Grease a 3-quart baking dish and alternate layers of bread, egg mixture, and cheese.

3. Allow to sit, covered, several hours or overnight in refrigerator.

4. Bake at 325°F for 1 hour.

Serves 4

Mrs. Dennis O'Toole's Incomprehensible and Utterly Impractical Irish Oatmeal

Difficulty Level: Beanbrain

On lunch break from their dog-washing business in *Mutts to You*, the Stooges find a baby abandoned on a doorstep. Naturally, they rescue the tyke, take him home, name him Butch, and feed and clothe him. The Stooges have a soft spot for kids.

Then the news breaks: a baby matching Butch's description has been kidnapped, and police have organized a manhunt for the culprits. The Stooges, realizing they have Butch, do what anyone would do in such a dangerous situation: they disguise Curly as Butch's mother, the sturdy Irish lass known as Mrs. Dennis O'Toole, and try to make a getaway.

As luck has it, the first person they stumble across is barrel-chested Irish policeman Officer O'Halloran, who is delighted to make Mrs. O'Toole's acquaintance. Charmed immediately, O'Halloran asks if the baby is still on the bottle.

"He don't smoke, drink, nor chew," Curly says indignantly.

Curly's Irish brogue is so convincing that Officer O'Halloran suspects nothing . . . until he sees the sponges stuffed inside Curly's pantyhose. After that, the jig is up for Mrs. Dennis O'Toole and her two sidekicks.

Stooge fans miss Mrs. Dennis O'Toole. This recipe, however, should help rekindle memories of that strapping Irish lassie with the lyrical accent and those beefy calves.

....

2 cups water

Pinch of salt

1 cup old-fashioned rolled oats

¼ cup brewed coffee, warm

1 teaspoon Irish whiskey, optional

1 tablespoon sugar

½ cup whipped cream or nondairy whipped topping

1. Combine the water and salt in a small saucepan. Bring water to a boil and stir in the oats. Cook over medium heat, stirring occasionally, for 5 minutes until thickened. Cover the pan to keep the oatmeal warm.

2. Combine the warm coffee, whiskey (if desired), and the sugar. Stir to dissolve the sugar. Pour warm oatmeal into serving bowls. Drizzle with the coffee mixture and stir it in. Spoon whipped cream on top to serve.

Makes 2 servings

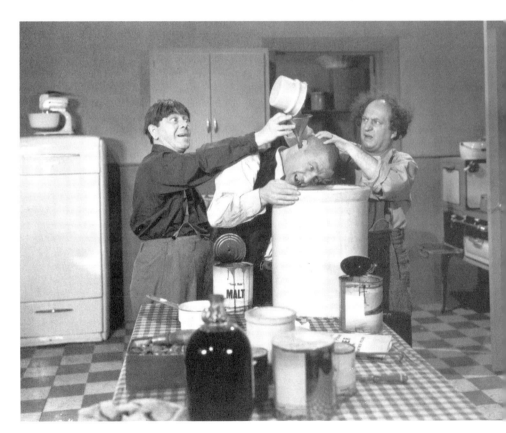

Whenever possible, filter your ingredients.

Gritto Grits

Difficulty Level: Rummy

Moe missed his calling. He should have been in broadcasting.
You can see it immediately in *Micro-Phonies*, where he
and fellow janitors Larry and Curly fiddle around in the radio
studio they are supposed to be cleaning. Moe takes to the
microphone like a natural, arching his eyebrows, tilting his
head dramatically, and bringing newfound zest to a soap
commercial:

> *Use Gritto, radio friends, the soap that gives
> your hands that dishpan look! How will the old
> man know you've been working if your hands
> don't have that dishpan look, hmm? Put a box
> of Gritto in a glass of water and listen to it fizz!
> Remember, Gritto spelled sideways is Ottri-
> guh . . . guh.*

So dramatic is Moe's reading that for years Stooge fans
scoured supermarkets in search of a box of Gritto. (Strangely,
no one has found any, even after spelling it for dumbfounded
clerks.) The following recipe is based on the deduction that
the active ingredient in Gritto must have been grits. Try Gritto
Grits, readers, and feel free to eat it with your hands for that
dishpan look.

• •

4 cups water

1 cup quick-cooking grits

¼ cup (½ stick) butter or margarine

½ teaspoon salt

1 cup milk

3 eggs, separated

1 cup shredded sharp cheddar cheese

Most accidents occur in the kitchen.

1. Preheat oven to 400°F. Grease a 1½-quart baking dish and set aside.

2. Bring the water to a boil in a medium saucepan. Stir in the grits, butter, and salt. Add the milk and reduce heat to medium–low. Cover the pan and cook for 5 to 7 minutes until creamy and soft. Remove the pan from the heat.

3. Beat the egg yolks and stir into the cooked grits, then stir in the cheese. Beat the egg whites until they are stiff and fold into the grits. Pour the mixture into the baking dish, spreading evenly. Bake for 25 to 30 minutes until set. Serve hot.

Makes 6 servings

French Toast from the Rue de Schlemiel

Difficulty Level: Bubblebrain

Curmudgeons moan that the Stooges are all about violence. Those who have watched *Love at First Bite* know that the opposite is true: the Stooges are all about love.

It was in Paris, on the Rue de Schlemiel, that Shemp wooed and won the heart of shapely French socialite Fifi. (When slick advertising executives invented the slogan, "Paris is for Lovers," they weren't contemplating the Eiffel Tower or the banks of the Seine; they were thinking only of Fifi and Shemp.)

Not everyone discovers love so romantically. But we all can toast the romance of Fifi and Shemp in the kitchen by preparing French Toast from the Rue de Schlemiel, an aromatic recipe of chivalry and seduction that proves, yet again, that the Stooges are all about love.

....

2 eggs

⅔ cup milk

½ teaspoon ground cinnamon

1–2 tablespoons butter or margarine

6 thick slices day-old white bread

1. Beat the eggs in a shallow dish with a fork. Beat in the milk and cinnamon.

2. Heat a griddle or large skillet over medium heat. Add 1 tablespoon of the butter to melt. Meanwhile, coat bread slices with the egg mixture on both sides. Brown the egg-dipped slices in the hot skillet about 2 minutes on each side, adding more butter to the skillet as needed.

3. Serve French toast warm with a fruit-flavored syrup.

Makes 3 servings

Chapter 5

Snacks

"It's only Curly. He never could stand green onions. They get in his hair—I mean his eyes."

Moe, explaining why Curly appears to be crying in *Mutts to You*

Porcupine Potatoes

Difficulty Level: Puddinhead

Every young boy grows up yearning for Larry's head of hair. Not for its power to attract beautiful women (though it splendidly accomplishes that goal for Larry). And not because it is so easy to pull (Larry would certainly prefer his hair to be less frequently pulled).

The real reason so many boys covet Larry's hair is for the nicknames.

Kids are tired of mundane monikers like "Lefty," "Junior" and "Scooter." Redheads have had enough of "Red."

But luck into a magnificent and bushy patch of thatch like Larry's, and the resplendent nicknames pour in: Mangy Floormop, Flatbush Flathead, Mophead, Nesthead, Hot Airedale, Porcupine. Especially Porcupine. All these nicknames are relished by Larry, and all were invented by a single admirer: Moe!

In honor of the world's fuzziest hairdo—and the nickname that made it grand—this recipe for Porcupine Potatoes is dedicated to all those who have crazy things coming out of their heads.

. . . .

1 package of frozen Ore-Ida hash brown potatoes

1 stick of butter or margarine

1 pint of half-and-half

1 large yellow onion, chopped

Salt and freshly ground black pepper to taste

1 large package of shredded mild cheddar cheese

1. Thaw the potatoes.

2. In a small saucepan, melt the butter. Combine butter and half-and-half in a shallow baking pan. Combine potatoes and onion and layer evenly in pan.

3. Bake potatoes for approximately 45 minutes at 350°F.

4. Remove the pan from the oven. Layer potatoes with cheese and bake until cheese is melted and browned on top.

Shopping for Staples at the Pinch Penny Market
• • • • • • • • • • • • • •

Take away Chef Curly's special ingredients and his Filet of Sole and Heel's no big deal, his Yankee Noodle Soup won't salute.

A well-stocked kitchen is essential to a great chef like Curly, and it's important to you, too. Load up on the following ingredients (all of which appear in Stooge films and are available at your local Pinch Penny Market), and you'll be ready at a moment's notice to prepare delicacies from Adam and Eve on a Raft to Woo-Woo-Woo-Woo Cheese Fondue. (See Index.)

Anacanapanasan

Anacanapon

Anapanacag

Anasanapacarscram

Bicarbonate of soda

Bretta

Cedascram

Cotton

Croomithistle

Ectowhozis (may substitute with Ectowhatsis)

Eenar

Eenginzoemen

Eenots

Falsyeth

Fine Powdered Alum

Gasoline

Jumbo Mexican Jumping Beans

Mishegas

Molasses

Papeeptoomin

Pickle juice

Piddledictatar

Pyareecon

Seltzer

Tabasco

Turpentine

200 percent wool (taken from sheep that led a double life)

Zendayfus

Filmy Watermelon

Difficulty Level: Useless

Ordinary recipes are not usually inspired by international crimes. But this is no ordinary cookbook, and Bortch is no ordinary criminal.

Bortch is perhaps the trickiest—and deadliest—fiend in the annals of Stooge crime. Warm and neighborly on the outside, the dashing foreign spy befriends the Stooges in *Dunked in the Deep* and *Commotion on the Ocean* . . . in order to facilitate the smuggling of top-secret microfilm he has hidden inside three delicious watermelons. The rat probably has no personal affection at all for the Stooges.

Neighbors don't always embrace the Stooges so readily, so Moe, Larry, and Shemp are naturally quite eager to assist Bortch. But soon enough they find themselves stowaways aboard a freighter bound for enemy waters.

No one could blame the Stooges had they decided to whimper and hide in a corner. But that is not the style of such heroic men. Instead, they get very hungry and decide to eat Bortch's watermelons, never suspecting that the balance of world power lies embedded in the fruit. Bortch, however, is incensed, and sets out to kill the three brave stowaways. Needless to say, Bortch doesn't last long, especially when Moe gets his hands on a cast-iron counterweight that does much to change the shape of Bortch's skull.

Varunu: Allow me to introduce myself. I am Varunu, witch doctor of this tribe.

Larry: What's cookin', doc?

Moe: Shut up. Don't give him any ideas.

Hula-La-La

The recipe for Filmy Watermelon is delicious and nutritious. Just remember to politely refuse if asked by any charming neighbors to carry it onto a strange ocean liner.

••

1 heaping quart seeded watermelon chunks,
about 1 inch thick, chilled

½ tablespoon unflavored gelatin

3 tablespoons cold water

¼ cup granulated sugar

3 tablespoons light corn syrup

2 tablespoons fresh lime juice

Mini chocolate chips, as needed

1. Puree the watermelon chunks in a food processor. When the fruit is smoothly blended, turn machine off but do not remove the fruit.

2. In a small bowl, sprinkle the gelatin over 3 tablespoons cold water and let it stand 2 minutes. Place the bowl into a microwave oven and heat for 30 seconds on high to melt the gelatin. Stir in the sugar, corn syrup, and lime juice.

3. With the food processor running, pour the gelatin mixture through the feed tube into the watermelon puree. Blend until the mixture is smooth.

4. Fill two empty ice cube trays with watermelon mixture. Sprinkle each cube of fruit with some mini chocolate chips and push the chips into the fruit. (Push microfilm into one of the fruit cubes, if desired.) Set the trays into the freezer until watermelon cubes are frozen.

Makes 32 watermelon cubes

Puppo Dog Biscuits

Difficulty Level: Picklepuss

Moe (inspecting dog bones Curly has served him): Say, is this my dinner?

Curly: Why soitenly! Fricaseed bone. It's delicious!

Moe: Since when do I look like a dog?

Curly: I don't know. I ain't seen you lately.

Calling All Curs

What a waste. The Stooges use Puppo Dog Biscuits to make fancy appetizers in *Crash Goes the Hash*, but not one of their elegant party guests so much as thanks them.

A dog, on the other hand, would be grateful for just a taste of a munchy, crunchy Puppo Dog Biscuit. Even wealthy dogs don't get snooty when it comes to delicious treats.

The Stooges have a special relationship with dogs, and even share a dinner table with them in *Calling All Curs*. Few men understand a dog's mind like the Stooges.

Puppo Dog Biscuits deserve to be enjoyed by those unpretentious souls who bark and roll over. You might decide to serve this recipe to regal dinner guests, but remember how rudely they behaved in *Crash Goes the Hash*: sometimes, a tuxedo is no replacement for a wet nose, droopy ears, and unconditional approval.

••

2 cups whole wheat flour

½ cup old-fashioned rolled oats

2 teaspoons instant beef bouillon

¾ cup hot water

3 tablespoons vegetable oil

1. Preheat oven to 325°F. Combine the flour and oats in a mixing bowl. Dissolve the instant bouillon in the hot water. Stir the bouillon and the oil into the flour mixture to form a stiff dough.

2. Roll out the dough into a circle ¼ to ½ inch thick. Using a bone-shaped cookie cutter, cut biscuits and put them on an ungreased cookie sheet.

3. Bake the biscuits for 45 minutes, or until crisp and dry. Cool on a wire rack. Store dog biscuits in a covered container.

Makes 12–14 biscuits

Joe Besser, master of the midnight snack

The Regal Tea and Crumpets of Lord Larryington and Sir Moeington

Difficulty Level: Cementhead

Let's reserve moral judgment for a moment on Moe and Larry's decision in *Heavenly Daze* to become con men, and instead inspect their technique.

> **Moe (to Curly, just before the Stooges attempt suicide):** Wait a minute! If you're going to bump yourself off, what's the idea of eating pie?
>
> **Curly:** So I can die-gest right!
>
> *Rhythm and Weep*

Dressed in dapper tuxedos and intent on selling a bogus fountain pen that writes under whipped cream, Moe and Larry affect majestic British accents and dub themselves Lord Larryington and Sir Moeington in order to emanate an air of nobility in front of the couple they intend to swindle.

When the whipped cream explodes and the fountain pen flies into Larry's forehead, the deal is blown and the Stooges are ruined. Had Moe and Larry prepared the traditional British snack of tea and crumpets, however, they might have had a chance to salvage the sale. Tea and crumpets soothe even the most savage souls.

....

1 envelope active dry yeast

¾ cup warm milk

1 tablespoon butter or margarine

1 teaspoon sugar

½ teaspoon salt

1 egg

1 cup flour

1. Dissolve the yeast in the warm milk in a medium bowl. Stir in the butter, sugar, salt, egg, and flour. Beat until smoothly blended. Cover the bowl and let the dough rise at room temperature for 1 hour or until doubled.

2. Grease a griddle or large skillet and set over medium heat. Grease the insides of several empty 6-ounce tuna fish cans, tops and bottoms removed. Set the can rings on the griddle and pour 2 tablespoons batter into each ring. Cook until bubbles break the surface, 1 to 2 minutes. Remove the rings and flip the crumpets over to brown the other side, 1 to 2 minutes. Repeat with the remaining batter.

3. Serve crumpets with jam or marmalade, if desired.

Makes 12 crumpets or 6 servings

Press, Press, Pull Pretzels

Difficulty Level: Knothead

Of all the ingenious schemes the Stooges devise to outwit authorities, none is more brilliant than the one they pull in *Three Little Beers*.

Denied entrance into the big golf tournament, Moe, Larry, and Curly duck into a nearby men's room and emerge moments later with sparkling credentials. Moe flashes a button that says "Press" and is allowed to enter. Larry flashes a button that says "Press" and is allowed to enter. Curly flashes a button that says "Pull," but he enters anyway.

Press, Press, Pull Pretzels celebrates the glory of the Stooges' refusal to take no for an answer. Prepare this recipe stubbornly and bring some along to a sold-out ball game; you never know when you'll need a delicious credential.

··

1 11-ounce can refrigerated breadstick dough

1 egg, beaten

½ to ¾ teaspoon coarse sea salt crystals

1. Preheat oven to 375°F.

2. Unroll the breadstick dough and separate at the perforations to form 8 strips. Twist each strip into a pretzel shape. Arrange them on a large ungreased cookie sheet. Paint the dough with the beaten egg, then sprinkle lightly with the salt crystals.

3. Bake in the oven until the crust is a deep golden brown, about 15 minutes. Serve the pretzels warm.

Makes 8 servings

Onion Oil's Full-Service Fluffy Popcorn

Difficulty Level: Softboiled Egghead

Fuller Grime is no fool.

As general manager of the Onion Oil Company in *Slaphappy Sleuths,* he vows to stop a string of baffling robberies at the company's service stations. His mission: to hire three "stupid-looking but brainy" detectives to crack the case. Claiming to be flexible on the brainy requirement, he hires detectives Moe, Larry, and Shemp to go undercover.

On the job, the Stooges provide customers with amenities not typically associated with gas stations. But the shaves, manicures, and squirts of cologne they administer cannot compare with the prodigious amounts of white, fluffy popcorn Shemp manages to coax from a restless radiator. (Sadly, the gas station is robbed from beneath their noses, but at least the Stooges aren't hungry when it happens.)

Stooges' Onion Oil's Full-Service Fluffy Popcorn

••

1 box popping corn

1 squeaky mechanic's oilcan
full of lubricating oil

1 overheating radiator

1 bottle of radiator sealant

Inspect radiator to make certain it is overheating. Reach for radiator sealant but mistakenly grab popping corn instead. Pour popping corn into radiator.

When rivers of white, fluffy popcorn gloriously erupt from radiator, stuff handfuls into hat and pockets. Use squeaky mechanic's oilcan to butter the popcorn to taste.

Another Full-Service Fluffy Popcorn

• •

¼ cup corn oil

½ cup yellow hulless popcorn

Popcorn salt to taste

Onion powder to taste

1. Pour the oil into the bottom of a medium saucepan and place the pan over medium heat for about 3 minutes. Add a couple of the popcorn kernels. When they pop, pour in the remaining kernels to cover the pan bottom evenly. Immediately, cover the pan and let the corn pop, shaking pan often. When the popping sound has nearly stopped, remove the pan from the heat to empty the popped corn into a large bowl.

2. Mix a little popcorn salt with an equal amount of onion powder in a small dish. Sprinkle it onto the hot, popped corn to taste, tossing to coat evenly. Eat popcorn warm.

Makes 2–4 servings

Always wash your hands before cooking.

Joe Besser's Five-Foot-Five by Five-Foot-Five Consolidated Fujiyama California Pizza Pies

Difficulty Level: Stupid Stooge

Blame it on boyish enthusiasm or blame it on greed. Joe would be the first one to admit that he made a mistake in *Quiz Whizz* by investing his $15,000 jackpot in Consolidated California Fujiyama Smog Bags. Especially given the suspicious initials of his business partners, R. O. Broad and G. Y. Prince.

> "Now you're getting your vitamins: starch, vegetables, hypochondriacs."
> Moe, to baby, in *Sock-A-Bye Baby*

Had Joe invested instead in pizza, he might have made millions. After all, his dimensions—as described by Moe—were perfect for such a venture: five-foot-five by five-foot-five.

∙∙

12 snack-size pita bread rounds
(2½-inch diameter)

¼ cup pizza sauce

½ cup shredded mozzarella cheese

1. To make each pizza snack, spread a pita round with 1 teaspoon of the sauce. Cover the sauce with 2 teaspoons of the shredded cheese. Place a single layer of the prepared rounds onto an aluminum pan that fits into a toaster oven.

2. Preheat a toaster oven to 500°F. Bake the pizza pitas for about 4 minutes or until the cheese is melted. Serve hot.

Makes 4 servings

Crabby Curly's Overstuffed Crabs

Difficulty Level: Mangy Floormop

You can't blame Curly for not liking crab. Just look what happens to him inside the royal palace in *Matri-Phony*.

Delighted to see a crab on a bountiful buffet, Curly joyously declares, "A tarantula!" Perhaps offended by this remark, the crab uses its sinister claw to steal an olive from Curly's plate . . . and to return the pit for good measure.

Naturally Curly is distressed by this larcenous crustacean, but his troubles are just beginning. The crab's next heist is Curly's pickle, which it uses to spray juice all over Curly's face. Like any innocent diner being ruthlessly tormented by a crab, Curly attacks his nemesis with a wooden mallet, then celebrates his victory by making a crab sandwich.

But the crab is not quite dead and proves it by crunching Curly's nose in its viselike grip until the two combatants drop to the floor in a full-blown brawl.

Such an incident should not discourage chefs, but it should remind them that certain ingredients do not always cooperate.

Stooges' Crabby Curly's Overstuffed Crabs

···

1 large crab (deceased)

2 lemon wedges

Falsely inform a friend that he has dropped a serviette. When friend looks down, smash crab on his head to separate legs and tail.

Mistake crab for a spider and refuse to eat. Tentatively inspect crab leg, remove the meat, and eat the shell. Remark, as Larry does to Moe, that you like crab, but do not like "the stuffing." Crunch the shells noisily, taking time between bites to squirt friend with lemon wedges.

After finishing crab leg shells, rise to leave the table. Appear astonished as your stomach rattles noisily, then hand tray of remaining empty shells to friend and instruct him to "have this crab refilled."

Another Crabby Curly's Overstuffed Crabs: Crab Spread

•••

8 ounces cooked crabmeat, picked over to remove cartilage

¼ cup mayonnaise

½ tablespoon fresh lemon juice

½ tablespoon Worcestershire sauce

½ teaspoon onion powder

Chopped parsley to taste

1. Mix the crabmeat with the mayonnaise, lemon juice, Worcestershire sauce, and onion powder in a bowl. Blend thoroughly. Add chopped parsley, as desired. Chill the spread in the refrigerator.

2. Spread the crabmeat mixture onto toast triangles to serve.

Makes 4–6 servings

Look at the Grouse!

Difficulty Level: Worm

There are some Stooge experiments no one should try at home. For example, it is never appropriate to test the sharpness of a saw by running that saw across the bald head of a friend.

But there are other Stooge experiments that amateurs may conduct safely, the most fascinating of which occurs in *Pop Goes the Easel.*

Moe is a master painter and poses his delicate model by instructing her to gaze skyward and look at the grouse. Curly, however, remarks that there are no grouse in the sky. After several inspiring blows to Curly's behind and noggin, the sky suddenly reveals its winged prize.

"Look at the grouse!" Curly exclaims.

This experiment works well whenever friends or loved ones don't see what you wish them to see. It also works wonders in the kitchen, when no one seems able to find a thing to eat. Simply apply a few well-placed kicks to a friend's hindquarters, stand back, and watch him declare, "Look at the grouse!" You'll know then that it is the perfect time to fix this experimental recipe.

Chicken Fingers

· ·

1 large (6-ounce) boneless, skinless
chicken breast half

2 teaspoons mustard

1 slice (1½ ounces) Swiss or mozzarella cheese

2 tablespoons dry bread crumbs

1. Preheat oven to 350°F.

2. Pound the chicken breast as thin as possible under plastic wrap without tearing the meat. Rub meat with the mustard, then lay the slice of cheese on it to cover the meat. Roll the chicken up around the cheese, starting with the long side of the meat. The rolled-up meat should resemble a fat cigar. Coat the roll completely in the bread crumbs and place on a flat baking pan.

3. Bake the chicken roll until browned and cooked through, about 20 minutes. Cut into 8 crosswise slices. Spear each slice with a toothpick to serve.

Makes 2 servings

The Stooges' dog proved to be a wonderful chicken thief, but they should have taught the mutt to share.

Joe's "Not So Hard!" Nachos

Difficulty Level: Titmouse

Like most of us, Joe dislikes pain. His trademark whine, "Not so *hard!*" speaks for generations of disaffected victims who constantly find their eyes on the receiving end of a pair of poking fingers.

Joe might seem a bit of a Milquetoast to some, but his pacifist nature pays big dividends in the kitchen. Try, for instance, to burn a steak or overbeat an egg while whimpering, "Not so *hard!*" Impossible, right?

> **"What a funny thing. It don't know whether it's coming or going!"**
> Curly, commenting on the tamale he is served in *Three Sappy People*

That is why Joe immediately inspires a nachos recipe. This traditional Mexican dish is often made too spicy for many eaters; with Joe's mollycoddle touch, however, even those with sensitive tongues won't sniffle, "Not so *hard!*"

• •

32 triangular yellow corn tortilla chips

1 cup shredded Monterey Jack cheese

32 mild pickled jalapeño slices, drained

Mild salsa

1. Preheat an oven broiler.

2. Arrange the chips close together in a single layer on a cookie sheet. Sprinkle the cheese evenly over the chips. Broil until the cheese melts and begins to brown, about 1 minute. Top each chip with a jalapeno slice.

3. Serve the nachos warm. Top with a spoonful of salsa, if desired.

Makes 2–3 servings

Chapter 6

Moe (to passerby on street): Hey, buddy. Pay me a little attention, will you? Lend me a dime for a hamburger.

Man: Go on, you can get a hamburger for a nickel anyplace.

Moe: I know, but I gotta have the other nickel for a bicarbonate of soda.

Three Little Pigskins

Larry: We can camp near a lake and catch all the fish we can eat. You know fish is great brain food.

Moe: You know, you should fish for a whale.

Pardon My Clutch

Lunch

Seasick Sausage

Difficulty Level: Moron

Shemp is a man's man. Just look at how he eats on a boat.

While Moe and Larry get seasick during a storm at sea in *Commotion on the Ocean*, Shemp celebrates the occasion by devouring three fistfuls of sausage.

"Delicious! If only I had some whipped cream!" Shemp declares.

Larry looks lily-livered. Moe looks emaciated.

"Oh, softies! Can't take it, eh? I'll eat it, don't worry about it. Ha ha ha ha!" cackles Shemp. "Gimme the high seas! Gimme the salty water! Oh, boy! Ha ha ha ha! They can't take it!"

Sausage is not good boat food, as Shemp himself soon discovers. Caution: do not eat this recipe aboard the high seas.

....

½ tablespoon olive oil

8 ounces mild or hot Italian sausage,
cut into 2 6-inch lengths

1 small green bell pepper, cut into thin strips

½ cup marinara sauce

2 6-inch Italian sandwich rolls, split

1. Heat the oil in a medium skillet over medium heat about 1 minute. When hot, add the sausage and bell pepper strips. Cook until the sausage pieces are browned, turning the meat and stirring the peppers occasionally, about 10 minutes. Add the marinara sauce, cover the pan, and reduce the heat to low. Simmer the mixture until sausage is thoroughly cooked, 5 to 7 minutes.

2. Meanwhile, warm the sandwich rolls in a toaster oven or microwave oven. Place the sausage and peppers, spooned with sauce, in the split rolls. Serve immediately.

Makes 2 servings

Hook, Line & Sinker's Tuna Fish Stinker

Difficulty Level: Spongehead

How could Hook, Line & Sinker have failed?

The Stooges' traveling fish business in *Cookoo Cavaliers* had it all—a catchy name, a smorgasbord of fish, and three singing salesmen.

It is true that Larry Hook, Moe Line, and Curly Sinker did not refrigerate their product, wore gas masks to handle inventory, and hurled fish to customers who lived in upper-story dwellings. But no business is perfect, and besides, where else might a fish lover hope to purchase bluefish and gefilte fish from the same truck?

> **"Must have been a flying fish . . ."**
> Curly, puzzled after a fish he was frying disappears from the pan in *Even as I.O.U*

Had customers been a bit more patient with Hook, Line & Sinker, perhaps we'd still be hearing the irresistible musical refrain that the Stooges used to hawk their tasty wares (sung by Moe—in catchy rhythm—with Curly and Larry dancing in step):

> *We have rock caught sea bass;*
> *Albacore and pickerool;*
> *Sand dab yellowtail;*
> *Tuna fish and mackerel;*
> *Bluefish, sailfish, half-and-half and if you wish,*
> *Swordfish, whitefish, herring, and gefilte fish!*
> (Curly and Larry)
> *And that ain't all!*

> **Bortch:** What have you got there?
> **Larry:** That's a dish of fish and it's perfect. You can take my word for it. On fish, I'm a common sewer!
> *Commotion on the Ocean*

Stooges' Hook, Line & Sinker's Tuna Fish Stinker

· ·

1 large tuna, unrefrigerated
(dead 30 days or more)

1 gas mask

1 car (must have trunk)

Wait until a blazing summer day, then place tuna securely in car trunk. Allow to sit for 48 hours or until neighbors call police. Drive around yelling, "Fresh fish!" from car window until a hungry person flags you down. Fasten gas mask to face, open trunk, and drop tuna onto a nearby flower bed. After flowers snap shut and wilt, beg fleeing customer to buy tuna anyway. Return home and cook tuna yourself.

Serves 1

Another Hook, Line & Sinker's Tuna Fish Stinker: Tuna Salad Sandwich

· ·

2 tablespoons chopped celery

1 tablespoon chopped green onion

1 6-ounce can chunk light tuna in water, drained

2 tablespoons mayonnaise

1/8–1/4 teaspoon lemon and pepper
seasoning salt

4 slices white sandwich bread

1. Combine the celery and onion in a small bowl. Add the drained tuna and mix well. Add the mayonnaise and blend. Season with lemon and pepper seasoning salt, adjusting to taste.

2. Spread the salad onto 2 bread slices. Cover sandwiches with the remaining bread. Cut each sandwich in half to serve.

Makes 2 servings

Limburger à la Larry

Difficulty Level: Mashed Potato Muscles

Moe often declared Limburger to be his "favorite fruit." Curly rubbed Limburger over his chest before making a grand entrance at a high-society party.

So why dedicate this book's only delicious Limburger recipe to Larry? Because it is Larry who, in *Cuckoo on a Choo Choo*, is so absorbed in his luscious Limburger sandwich that he barely notices the skunk that has crawled atop Shemp's head.

That is how true Limburger lovers love Limburger. That is why this recipe could only be called Limburger à la Larry.

Stooges' Limburger à la Larry

1 brick Limburger

2 slices burned toast

1 phony beard (preferably knee-length)

Leave Limburger in the sun for 48 hours until edges turn pale shade of green. Spread on burned toast, then twist toast clockwise to lock sandwich together.

Eat sandwich. Fasten phony beard to chin and return to work confident that you will not be recognized.

Another Limburger à la Larry: Limburger Sandwich

• •

4 slices rye sandwich bread

1 tablespoon butter

8 thin slices sweet onion

3 ounces Limburger cheese, sliced

½ apple, peeled, cored, sliced thin

1. Divide and spread the butter on each slice of the bread.

2. For each sandwich, arrange half the onion slices on one slice of bread and cover it with half the cheese slices. Top with half the apple slices and cover the sandwich with the remaining slice of bread, buttered-side down. Press on the sandwich to hold it together. Cut sandwiches in half to serve.

Makes 2 servings

> "My sandwich bit me; I'm beating it into submission."
>
> Curly, explaining why he is barking at and pummeling his sandwich in *Calling All Curs*

Gastronomic Names

Just watching the Stooges makes you hungry.

Not only because they prepare such scrumptious meals, but because so many of the people and places they encounter are so deliciously named.

Browse this list of mouth-watering monikers that have appeared in Stooges films, and see if your stomach doesn't begin to rumble.

People

Abel Lamb Stewer

Antonio Zucchini Salami Gorgonzola de Pizza

Castor and Earle Revue

Doctor Ba Loni Sulami

Doctors Hart, Burns, and Belcher

Field Marshall Herring

Garçon (canine)

The Great Svengarlic

Hammond Egger

Hilarious Hash Slingers

I. M. Greecy

Mattie Herring

Panther Brewing Co.

Pinch Penny Market

Professor Frankfurter

Steelia Pumpernickel

Bars, Taverns, and Saloons

Black Louie's Pirate Den

Double Deal's Five "D" Delight

Felix Stout's Bar

Longhorn Saloon

Maxey's Place

Peaceful Gulch Saloon

Red Dog Saloon

Rite Bar

Storey's Saloon

Businesses/Products

Cantina De Rosa

Mrs. Throttlebottom's Chicken Coop

No Burpoline Gasoline

Onion Oil Company

Seabiscuit Food Corp.

Places, Destinations, Kingdoms, and Faraway Lands

Bay of Rum

Coleslawvania

Rhum Boogie

Smorgasbord Castle

South Starv-Vania

Starvania

Wienerschnitzel Straza

Restaurants

Black Bottom Café

Café Casbahbah

Café La-Mer-Essen

Elite Café

Flounder Inn

Jive Café

Joe's Beanery

O'Brien's Kosher Restaurant

Squid McGuffey's Café

Vesuvius Restaurant

Ye Colonial Inn

Coney Island Curly's Cornpone Corn Dogs

Difficulty Level: Pebblebrain

Badlands Blackie has killed the last six sheriffs of Dead Man's Gulch. Worse, he's kidnapped the lovely Nell's pappy and won't release him until Nell consents to become Mrs. Blackie.

Ordinary lawmen would flee from such a hopeless situation. But in *The Three Troubledoers*, three mysterious figures emerge from the dusty shadows. Two become deputies of Dead Man's Gulch. The third becomes the new sheriff, Coney Island Curly.

Coney Island Curly's facility with a six-shooter looks certain to earn him an early grave, and it's difficult to determine whether his triple-thick bifocals help or hinder his terrible aim.

But Coney Island Curly possesses what the other sheriffs do not: the love of the beautiful Nell. Disguised as a justice of the peace, Curly disrupts the shotgun wedding of Blackie and Nell by reciting the unfamiliar vow, "Do you take this horse collar for your lawfully wedded harness?"

Such gallantry belongs to a bygone era. But for a taste of that Old West chivalry, prepare this recipe for Coney Island Curly's Cornpone Corn Dogs. And remember: It takes a man as brave as Coney Island Curly to eat 'em.

••

1 8½-ounce box corn muffin mix

1 egg

⅓ cup milk

4 jumbo all-beef hot dogs

1. Preheat oven to 400°F. Grease an 8-inch cast-iron skillet and set it aside.

2. Empty the contents of the box into a mixing bowl. Stir in the egg and milk to form a batter. It will be a little lumpy. Pour the batter evenly into the greased skillet. Cut the hot dogs in half crosswise, then push them into the cornmeal batter arranged like the spokes of a wheel.

3. Set the skillet into the oven to bake 20 to 25 minutes until corn bread is golden brown. Let the pan cool. Cut into wedges between each hot dog to serve.

Makes 8 servings

"Here, Fido; come back!"
Moe, after the hot dog he is about
to eat jumps onto the carpet and
scampers away in *Income Tax Sappy*

Señorita Cucaracha's Shrill Falsetto Tacos

Difficulty Level: Empty Skull

Opera buffs relish *Micro-Phonies*, the classic Stooge film in which Curly uses flowing gowns, a lovely bonnet, and a 78-RPM recording of "Voices of Spring" to transform himself into dainty diva Señorita Cucaracha.

The Señorita's glory, however, is snuffed out by a jealous tenor named Signor, who unplugs the Stooges' phonograph and fires a banana into Curly's mouth, exposing the Señorita as more musically challenged than she had earlier appeared.

Such an inelegant turn of events is disastrous for music lovers, but it does coax the viewer's appetite into action; watching all that flying fruit makes a Stooge fan hungry.

**Señorita Cucaracha and her two accompanists,
Señors Mucho (Larry) and Gusto (Moe)**

This recipe honors the accomplishments of Señorita Cucaracha, and should dampen the hunger pangs that inevitably attend a viewing of *Micro-Phonies*. Just be careful to prepare it in the privacy of your own dwelling; early testing of the recipe caused even tone-deaf chefs to spread their arms, drop to one knee, and perform the aria to "Voices of Spring."

· ·

1 pound lean ground beef

⅓ cup dried taco seasoning mix

⅔ cup water

8 packaged taco shells

1 cup shredded cheddar or Monterey Jack cheese

2 cups shredded iceberg lettuce

1 cup diced tomatoes

Taco sauce to taste

1. Brown the ground beef in a medium skillet over medium heat, stirring to break up any clumps of meat. Add the taco seasoning mix and the water. Bring the mixture to a simmer, then reduce heat to low and cook until thickened, 4 to 5 minutes. Remove the skillet from the heat.

2. Fill each taco shell by layering with seasoned beef, cheese, lettuce, and tomatoes. Serve the taco sauce on the side.

Makes 8 servings

Dr. Ba Loni Sulami's
Bait-and-Switch Love Sandwich

Difficulty Level: Little Man

You'd think that witch doctors in deepest Africa would have better things to do than invent love candy. But that's precisely what Dr. Ba Loni Sulami is up to in *Three Missing Links*.

Subjecting his love candy to none of the rigors demanded by American science, Sulami allows the untested potion to fall into the hands of Curly, who happens to be in Africa starring as a gorilla in the latest Hollywood blockbuster.

Curly's a natural in the role, so it comes as little surprise when a real gorilla shows up and immediately becomes jealous. Curly, demonstrating a remarkable ability to think while wearing a gorilla costume, offers Sulami's candy to the ape as a peace offering, then eats it himself in a show of good faith. Had the candy been properly tested, Curly might never have uttered to the confused gorilla those regrettable words, "Darling. I love you! Give me a little kiss!"

Test this bologna and salami sandwich first by asking a friend to stand nearby. Eat only a nibble. If no waves of mad, passionate attraction flood over you, feel safe to consume the rest. If, however, your friend begins to look like the love of your life, promptly hide in a gorilla costume and consume no more.

••

2 tablespoons mayonnaise

4 slices white sandwich bread

1 cup coarsely shredded iceberg lettuce

4 slices (4 ounces) bologna

6 thin slices (2 ounces) salami

1. Divide and spread the mayonnaise on each slice of bread.

2. For each sandwich, cover one slice of bread with some of the lettuce. Layer it with one slice of the bologna, 3 slices of the salami folded into halves, and a second bologna slice. Top the meat with some more of the lettuce and cover the sandwich with a bread slice, mayonnaise-side down. Press on the sandwich to hold it together.

3. Cut sandwiches in half and serve.

Makes 2 servings

Moe: Say, could I have a nice salami sandwich smothered in sour cream with cherry jelly?

Joe: Pickle in the middle and mustard on top?

Placing a down-to-earth lunch order while being held captive on the planet Sunev in *Outer Space Jitters*

Double Deal Decker's Double-Decker PB&J

Difficulty Level: Goosebrain

The saloon's chalkboard in *Horses' Collars* tells a morbid tale. Decker 117, Opponents 0. Ruthless cattle rustler Double Deal Decker has just plugged two more adversaries, and it looks like there ain't a lawman in the Wild West who can stop him.

But back at the Hyden Zeke Detective Agency, three brave gumshoes intend to change Decker's wicked ways. Their marksmanship is discouraging and they struggle with issues of bravery, but detectives Moe, Larry, and Curly vow to bring down the dirty Decker. Their secret weapon: Curly. And a mouse.

Mice drive Curly crazy. It's Decker's bad luck that there's a mouse around when the Stooges mosey into town.

The new score: Decker 117, the Stooges 1.

In the spirit of sportsmanship, this double-decker peanut butter and jelly sandwich is dedicated to Double Deal Decker. Just don't invite any mice.

• •

½ cup creamy peanut butter

4 heaping tablespoons grape jelly

6 slices white sandwich bread

2 bananas, sliced very thin

1. Combine the peanut butter and jelly in a bowl. Stir it one or two times to swirl the jelly into the peanut butter without mixing. It should look marbled.

2. Spread each of the bread slices with the swirled peanut-butter-and-jelly mixture, dividing equally. Arrange a quarter of the banana slices in an overlapping layer onto two slices of spread bread. Cover each with a bread slice, spread-side up.

Arrange the remaining banana slices over these top slices, and cover the sandwiches with the remaining two bread slices, spread-side down. Press on the sandwiches to hold them together.

3. Cut sandwiches in half and serve.

Makes 2 servings

Hammond Egger's Ham-Fisted Ham Sandwich

Difficulty Level: Dimwit

The Stooges didn't invent political treachery, but they added a mighty big chapter in *Three Dark Horses*.

Paid by shady pollsters to become delegates for presidential candidate Hammond Egger, the Stooges take instantly to politics, subscribing to slogans such as "A Chicken in Every Pot with Egger" and "Cuddle Up a Little Closer with Egger." They even anticipate themselves receiving high-ranking government appointments such as Secretary of the Offense, Secretary of the Inferior, and Toastmaster General.

But at the eleventh hour, something turns rotten with the Stooges. Moe begins to carry a sign that reads "Don't Be a Muttonhead—Vote for Abel Lamb Stewer," and within hours, the Stooges complete the double cross by casting their ballots for Egger's rival.

Stooge fans who value loyalty still haven't come to terms with *Three Dark Horses*. Food enthusiasts, however, realize that men of taste will always opt for lamb stew over ham and eggs. But in tribute to Hammond Egger, who, after all, was wronged by the Stooges, this recipe for a ham-fisted ham sandwich is presented in unimpeachable glory.

1 cup minced or ground ham

3–4 tablespoons chopped pimiento-stuffed olives

3 tablespoons mayonnaise

8 slices white sandwich bread, lightly toasted

1. Combine the ham and olives in a bowl. Add the mayonnaise and blend thoroughly.

2. Divide the deviled ham mixture evenly among 4 toast slices. Spread evenly. Cover each sandwich with another toast slice.

3. Cut sandwiches in half and serve.

Makes 4 servings

Judge: Order, order!

Curly: Order? I'll take a ham sandwich.

Judge: Hold thy tongue!

Curly: Not tongue—ham!

Back to the Woods

Burritos Muy Scrumptias de los Señors Mucho y Gusto

Difficulty Level: Chiseler

Legendary soprano Señorita Cucaracha (Curly, dressed in magnificent bonnet and flowing gown) deservedly gets much of the attention in *Micro-Phonies*. After all, it is the Señorita who possesses the soaring soprano and thrilling facial expressions.

But she could not have impressed the experts so convincingly without her two virtuoso accompanists, Señors Mucho (Larry) and Gusto (Moe). Always gentlemanly and protective of their charge (Moe and Larry expertly fire fruit into the mouth of a rival performer), Señors Mucho and Gusto are remembered here with a scrumptious burrito recipe that should make even the most tone-deaf cook sing like a diva.

....

1 12-inch flour tortilla

½ cup cooked rice

⅓ cup canned, drained beans

½ cup finely shredded iceberg lettuce

⅓ cup shredded carrot

½ cup chopped cooked chicken or pork

2 tablespoons mild or hot salsa

¼ cup shredded cheddar cheese

1. Soften the tortilla by wrapping it in a towel, then warming in a microwave oven on high for 20 to 30 seconds.

2. Lay the warm tortilla out flat. While it is still soft, layer each of the filling ingredients onto the center, starting with the rice and ending with the cheese. Roll the tortilla up tightly to enclose the filling.

Makes 1 serving

Kitchen utensils are not toys.

Enchanted, Enraptured, and Embalmed Enchiladas

Difficulty Level: Turniphead

Before the film *Half-Wits Holiday*, it was believed that gentlemen were born, not made. But soon after the Stooges took lessons in high culture from Professor Quackenbush and his dazzling daughter Lulu, Moe, Larry, and Curly attain levels of gentlemanliness so lofty that even the Windsors were heard to swoon.

> **"I'm too pleasingly plump as it is."**
> Curly, explaining candidly why he needs to lose a few pounds in *Flat Foot Stooges*

Professor Quackenbush has reason to be confident in his three protégés. Dressed for the society ball in splendid black tuxedos, the Stooges reassure him thusly:

Curly: Professor Quackenbush, have no qualms or trepidations.

Larry: We will justify your faith in us indubitably, sir.

Moe: Professor, the vicissitudes we have encountered have elevated us to a lofty position.

Soon thereafter occurred a thrillingly regal introduction. Upon being introduced to the genteel Mrs. Gottrocks and the ornate Countess Schpritzwasser, the Stooges make their fanciest impression of the evening:

Moe (bowing): Enchanted.
Larry (bowing): Enraptured.
Curly (bowing): Embalmed!

To honor newcomers to nobility, this little-known recipe for Enchanted, Enraptured, and Embalmed Enchiladas is most humbly presented. Its vicissitudes will elevate any diner to a lofty position.

• •

8 ounces mild chorizo sausage or
spiced pork sausage

1 cup canned refried beans

1 10-ounce jar or can enchilada sauce

8 corn tortillas

2 cups Mexican-style Chihuahua
shredded cheese

1. Remove the sausage from its casing and brown the meat in a
skillet over medium heat. Use a spatula to break up any
clumps. Drain off fat from the skillet and add the refried
beans to the meat.
Cook and stir over low
heat until mixture is
thoroughly hot, about 3
minutes. Remove from
the heat and set filling
aside.

> "Listen, you! If I'm gonna work like
> a horse, I'm gonna eat like one!"
>
> Curly, explaining to Moe why he has
> stopped pulling the Stooges' broken-
> down car and begun to eat a colossal
> sandwich in *G.I. Wanna Home*

2. Preheat oven to 350°F.
Ladle ½ cup of the
enchilada sauce into
the bottom of a
medium baking dish.

3. Soften the tortillas by wrapping them in foil and setting into
the oven for a couple of minutes to warm.

4. While the tortillas are still warm and soft, spread each with
2 tablespoons of the filling, then sprinkle with 2 tablespoons
of the cheese. Roll the tortillas up to enclose the filling and
place them in the baking dish, seam-side down. Ladle the
remaining sauce over the tortillas and sprinkle with the
remaining cheese.

5. Bake until the cheese is melted and the filling is hot, about 20
minutes.

Makes 8 servings

Moe, Larry, the (Grilled) Cheese!

Difficulty Level: Onionhead

Cheese is a versatile food, but before Curly, few realized it could be used to fight crime.

In *Horses' Collars*, Curly goes berserk at the very sight of a mouse. No one in the path of his flying fists, furious feet, or bucking belly is safe . . . until he eats some cheese.

"Moe, Larry, the cheese!" Curly cries, and his partners rush forth to save the day with a hunk of roquefort, Camembert, even Limburger.

(No one explains why Curly acts this way, though Moe provides some insight when he remarks that, "His father was a rat.")

It looks like curtains for the Stooges when murderous gunslinger Double Deal Decker and his henchmen prepare Moe, Larry, and Curly for the gallows. But a mouse moseys by, Curly goes crazy, and the day is saved . . . after Curly gets his cheese.

....

2 tablespoons soft butter

4 slices white sandwich bread

½ tablespoon Dijon mustard

⅔ cup shredded Swiss cheese

1. Use 1 tablespoon of the butter to spread onto each bread slice, then spread with a thin layer of mustard. Divide the cheese between two bread slices and cover the sandwiches with the remaining two slices, spread-side down.

2. Melt the remaining tablespoon of butter in a skillet over medium–low heat. Add the sandwiches and cover the pan. Cook about 2 minutes until golden brown on the undersides. Flip the sandwiches over and re-cover the pan. Cook about 2 minutes longer to brown, then remove sandwiches from the skillet.

3. Cut each sandwich in half and serve warm.

Makes 2 servings

Sloppy Moes

Difficulty Level: Musclebound

What a paradoxical name for a recipe. If there is one Stooge who stands for neatness, it's Moe.

Take Moe's hair. Always combed and with perfect sugar-bowl bangs, Moe's hairdo is a masterpiece of tidiness.

And Moe dresses immaculately. Even while sleeping, he wears a fully pressed suit of clothes under his sleeping gown.

Furthermore, Moe's punishments are clean. His seltzer bottle blasts leave little mess, and he seems careful to make an orderly disposal of whatever hair he pulls from Larry's head.

Sloppy Moes are named after Moe not because he's sloppy, but because they are perfect for Moe-style throwing. Messy on the inside but with a grippable bun, Sloppy Moes explode on contact and persuade misbehaving friends to fall into order. This recipe, more than any other, is ideal for use as a disciplinary tool.

* * *

1 pound lean ground beef

2 teaspoons onion powder

½ teaspoon dry mustard

1 jar (15½ ounces) sloppy joe sauce

1 tablespoon Worcestershire sauce

6 hamburger or sandwich buns

1. Brown the beef in a medium skillet over medium heat. Use a spatula to break up any clumps of meat. Stir in the onion powder and dry mustard. Pour in the sloppy joe sauce and stir in the Worcestershire. Bring the mixture to a simmer and cook until heated through.

2. Scoop the meat mixture onto the bun bottoms and cover sandwiches with bun tops to serve. Eat these over a large plate to catch spills.

Makes 6 servings

Larry's Leave-It-to-Cleaver Frankfurters

Difficulty Level: Nitwit

Dogs and cats love the kitchen, especially when a chef like Larry whips up his divinely aromatic specialties.

But pets must understand the rules of cooking before being allowed near the food. Especially in a restaurant like the one that employs Larry in *Rumpus in a Harem*.

Cats should not steal hot dogs intended for guests. Dogs should not howl loudly while the chef is using a meat cleaver to cut steaks.

Restaurant patron Hassan Ben Sober overreacted to the noises made by Chef Larry's pets when he threatened to behead Larry with a saber. But the lesson is clear: while preparing any recipe in this book, please keep the pets away from the customers.

Stooges' Larry's Leave-It-to-Cleaver Frankfurters
••

½ dozen frankfurters

1 oversized meat cleaver

After diners are seated next to kitchen, turn your back while your pet cat steals frankfurters. Chase cat into dining room, yelling "Scat!" and waving meat cleaver homicidally. After catching the cat, shake cleaver menacingly at it in front of diners, then return to kitchen. Disregard horrified expressions on customers' faces.

Chop frankfurters in kitchen without realizing that cat is playfully screeching every time the meat cleaver falls. Next, chase mischievous pet dog past diners, retrieve, and chop more frankfurters in kitchen while dog barks.

Serve plate of frankfurters to diners, who look as if they've seen a ghost. In the event one diner holds a saber to your throat and insists that you eat the food, sit down joyously, as Larry does, and declare, "When it comes to cooking, I'm the cat's meow!"

Another Leave-It-to-Cleaver Frankfurters:
Hot Dogs with Chili and Cole Slaw

8 all-beef hot dogs

1 15-ounce can beanless chili

8 hot dog buns, warmed and split

½ cup finely chopped onion

1 cup creamy cole slaw

1. Bring a saucepan of water to a simmer. Add the hot dogs, cover the pan, and cook over medium–low heat until heated through, about 5 minutes.

2. Meanwhile, heat the chili in a covered dish in a microwave oven on high for about 3 minutes, or until hot.

3. To make each sandwich, put a steamed hot dog into a warm bun. Top it with 2 tablespoons of the chili, 1 tablespoon of the chopped onion, and 2 tablespoons of the cole slaw. Serve warm.

Makes 8 servings   **Gentleman diners never reach.**

Shemp's Heep-Heep-Heeping Corned Beef Sandwich

Difficulty Level: Lunkhead

In the animal kingdom, no creature ever possessed a more unique cry of distress than Shemp.

"Heep-heep-heep-heep! Heep-heep-heep-heep-heep!"

His high-pitched screech usually signals the presence of a homicidal ghost, a furious policeman, a jealous husband. Around the dinner table, it could mean that the roast turkey has leaped off the table and begun to walk away.

This recipe for a heep-heep-heeping corned beef sandwich provides enough extra calories and carbohydrates to allow anyone to yelp "Heep-heep-heep." But use it sparingly; you do not want to become known in cooking circles as the chef who cried "Heep-heep-heep."

. . . .

1 cup coarsely chopped corned beef

1 teaspoon grated onion with juice

2 tablespoons finely chopped sweet pickle

¼ cup mayonnaise

6 slices rye sandwich bread, lightly toasted

1. Combine the corned beef with the grated onion and any collected onion juice in a bowl. Stir in the sweet pickle. Add the mayonnaise and stir to blend.

2. Spread the sandwich filling onto 3 slices of the toasted bread. Cover sandwiches with the remaining toast slices. Cut each sandwich in half to serve.

Makes 3 servings

Chapter 7

Soups and Salads

Cackle Soup

Difficulty Level: Numbskull

Snobby Parisian chefs have failed to appreciate the culinary skills of the great Chef Curly.

Some insist that cooks should never throw desserts at dinner guests. Others sneer at the delightful songs he sings while cooking.

But mention Curly's delicious Cackle Soup, and even the most finicky French chef would sell his soul for the divine chicken broth recipe.

You can watch Curly prepare this treat in *Busy Buddies*, but his secrets might escape you. Read below, however, and you'll be able to whip up the scrumptious treat as if you were the head chef at the Stooge-owned Jive Café.

Moe is not pleased with Chef Curly's Cackle Soup.

Stooges' Cackle Soup

••

1 skinny chicken

1 soup bowl

1 pot of boiling water

Place skinny chicken over soup bowl. Pour boiling water into skinny chicken. Wring skinny chicken's legs furiously while singing, "La-lee, la-la-lee!" Slide steaming bowl dangerously across table to serve.

Another Cackle Soup: Chicken and Vegetable

••

1 fat chicken (cut into pieces)

1 large yellow onion, peeled

2 large carrots, scraped and sliced thick

2 celery stalks

Salt and pepper to taste

Dry heel of rye bread (optional)

1. Bring four quarts of water to boil over medium heat. Add chicken and all other ingredients except carrots. Place lid halfway on pot, then lower flame to a strong simmer. Let simmer for 45 minutes, skimming fat from top every 10 minutes with a dry heel of rye bread or spoon.

2. Remove celery stalks when limp and onion when soft. Add salt and pepper to taste.

3. Drop carrots into the pot, being careful not to splash. Simmer for 20 to 30 minutes more. Test carrots with a fork for softness. Skim fat again.

Makes 6 servings

Professor Snead's Top-Secret Rocket Fuel

Difficulty Level: Matzohead

For decades, men have coveted Larry Fine's magnificent head of hair. Yet that proud, bushy mane is nearly the death of the Stooges in *Fuelin' Around*, where Larry is mistaken for Professor Snead, inventor of a top-secret rocket fuel and himself the owner of a miniforest atop his dome.

Three fiendish spies from the state of Anemia kidnap Larry, thinking him to be Professor Snead. Their sole demand: the secret formula. Or the Stooges die.

Larry tries hard, but science is not his best subject. His concoction turns out to burn holes through floors and cause jeeps to fly like airplanes. Prepare this recipe with vigor, but don't eat too much; Professor Snead's Top-Secret Rocket Fuel causes heartburn that will be a secret to no one.

Stooges' Professor Snead's Top-Secret Rocket Fuel

• •

½ pint of ectowhozis (may substitue with ectowhatsis)

4 grams of alkabob

1 shishkabob

1 jigger of sastrophonia

1 beaker carbolic acid

1 squirt of haratang

Combine all ingredients in large glass jug until mixture is smoking, hissing, and popping. Use siphon to recklessly pour mixture down shirtsleeve of unsuspecting friend until you hear a blood-curdling scream. Add a bit more carbolic acid. Test by sprinkling formula in a circle around the spot on which you stand. If mixed properly, the rocket fuel will cause the floor to collapse and you will plummet into the basement. Enjoy.

Another Rocket Fuel: Chili

. . . .

1 small yellow onion, chopped

2 garlic cloves, chopped

1 teaspoon vegetable oil

1 pound lean ground beef

½ tablespoon seasoned salt

1 tablespoon chili powder

1 15-ounce can tomato sauce

1 15-ounce can spicy chili beans

1 14½-ounce can stewed tomatoes

½ cup dark beer or stout

1. Cook the onion and garlic with the oil in a dutch oven over medium heat until softened, about 5 minutes. Add the ground beef. Use a spatula to break up any clumps, and brown the meat. Stir in the seasoned salt and chili powder.

2. Open the cans of tomato sauce, chili beans, and stewed tomatoes. Add them to the meat mixture. Do not drain. Stir in the beer. Cook the chili over low heat for 45 minutes to 1 hour until thickened to the desired consistency.

3. Serve chili with oyster crackers and hot sauce, if desired.

Makes 6 servings

This guard, who desires the recipe for Professor Snead's Top-Secret Rocket Fuel, should know that you can't rush greatness.
. . . .

Soapy Soup

Difficulty Level: Birdbrained Idiot

Raiding the refrigerator is the babysitter's greatest joy. Yet most babysitters remain conservative while on the job, settling for a peanut butter sandwich, a dish of ice cream, or some other humdrum snack.

Not Shemp. While on duty with Moe and Larry in *Baby Sitters Jitters*, Shemp boldly pursues his appetite for hot soup. The complicated ingredients and intricate instructions don't bother him in the least.

The fact that the soup causes the Stooges to blow prodigious amounts of bubbles should not discourage anyone from trying this recipe . . . so long as they can tell better than Shemp can the difference between soup and soap.

Stooges' Soapy Soup

· ·

1 box powdered soup

1 box powdered soap

1 cup water

⅞ ounce dried sage

Cinnamon

Mustard

Cloves

Baking powder

Reach for box of powdered soup, but accidentally grab powdered soap instead. Dump contents into a pan, then add water, sage, cinnamon, and mustard. Stare in amazement at box of cloves, mistake them for "gloves," then marvel, as Shemp does, at how the manufacturer manages to fit so many tiny mittens into a little spice box. Fumble around for baking powder, read the label, then declare in your best Shemp voice, "Powdered bacon; what'll they think of next?"

After allowing mixture to boil, serve in soup bowls and rub hands greedily in anticipation. Slurp loudly, then allow a friend to declare that the soup tastes like a dead horse. Reply, as Shemp did, by muttering, "You know, if I hadn't made this myself, I'd swear there was a little soap in it." Proceed to cough up enough soapy bubbles to fill a bathtub.

Another Soapy Soup: Corn Chowder

....

2 tablespoons butter or margarine

2 tablespoons flour

2 tablespoons minced green onion

2 tablespoons minced celery

1 tablespoon cooked, minced bacon

1 8¾-ounce can whole-kernel corn, drained

1 8½-ounce can cream-style corn, undrained

¾ cup canned chicken broth

1½ tablespoons sherry

¾ cup half-and-half

Pinch of ground nutmeg

Salt and freshly ground black pepper to taste

1. Melt the butter in a medium saucepan over low heat. Add the flour and stir to blend. Cook, stirring, for 2 minutes. Do not brown the mixture. Add the onion, celery, and bacon. Cook and stir 2 minutes to soften the vegetables. Add the drained corn and the cream-style corn. Pour in the broth and the sherry, and bring the mixture to a boil. Reduce the heat and simmer for 5 minutes.

2. Pour in the half-and-half. Heat just until hot; do not boil. Season the soup with nutmeg, salt, and pepper. Serve immediately.

Makes 3–4 servings

Cedric the Clam's Clam Chowder

Difficulty Level: Flatbush Flathead

No food is more dangerous than a smart-aleck shellfish.

Take Cedric, Larry's pet clam in *He Cooked His Goose*. Larry claims that Cedric is the only trained clam in the world, and sure enough, Cedric proves it by snapping seven times when asked the number of days in a week.

But Cedric reveals a troubling side to his personality after Larry asks, "Cedric, what do we do if we don't like somebody?" Rather than do the gentlemanly thing and keep silent, Cedric instead sprays Shemp in the face with a blast of water. It's no wonder that Shemp finally threatens, "Listen you, I'll get you in a chowder one day and look out, believe me!"

A chowder is a fine idea for a sassy clam, but it is not without pitfalls. In *Dutiful but Dumb*, the larcenous oyster in Curly's stew succeeds in stealing crackers and biting Curly's finger until poor Curly is forced to open fire on the bowl with his pistol.

Because of such unfortunate incidents, it is important to warn cooks to approach the following recipe with extreme caution.

Stooges' Cedric the Clam's Clam Chowder

• •

1 pair galoshes

1 yellow raincoat

1 ornery clam

1 packet clam powder

10 oyster crackers

1 pistol

Bring 1 gallon of water to boil and then stir in clam powder. Pour mixture into large soup bowl. Then drop one ornery clam into mixture.

Place one cracker into soup, then turn your attention elsewhere. Look back into the soup bowl and discover that your cracker is missing. Repeat until extremely frustrated. Investigate by wiggling finger inside the bowl. Scream in agony as the clam bites your finger and refuses to let go. After finally separating clam from finger, use pistol to shoot chowder in self-defense.

Another Clam Chowder

....

2 tablespoons diced salt pork or bacon

½ cup finely chopped onion

1 cup diced peeled potato

1 cup water

2 6½-ounce cans minced clams, undrained

1 cup half-and-half

Salt and ground white pepper to taste

Paprika to taste

1. Brown the salt pork in a saucepan over low heat until crispy, stirring often. Remove the crisped bits and reserve.

2. Add the onion to the saucepan, then add the potato and the water. Bring the liquid to a simmer, cover the pan, and cook until the potatoes are tender, 8 to 10 minutes.

3. Return the crisped salt pork to the saucepan. Stir in the clams with their juice, and return liquid to a simmer. Add the half-and-half. Heat just until hot; do not boil. Season the soup with salt and white pepper.

4. Sprinkle paprika on each bowl of hot soup. Serve with oyster crackers, if desired.

Makes 4 servings

Yankee Noodle Soup

Difficulty Level: Dewhead

> "This soup is a marvelous accomplishment, it's a prodigious achievement, you're gonna love it, it's putrid!"
>
> Curly, describing the Stooge-made Yankee Noodle Soup in *Nutty But Nice*

The glory days of restaurants—meaning the days when waiters still sang—are gone. But the legacy lives on through the Hilarious Hash Slingers, three singing waiters who bill themselves as "America's Gift to Indigestion" and who croon this irresistible recommendation in *Nutty but Nice*:

(Sung to the tune of "Yankee Doodle Dandy")

Our Yankee Noodle Soup is good;
You'll find it is no phony;
If you don't care for noodle soup,
We'll serve you macaroni!

1 tablespoon butter or margarine

⅓ cup chopped onion

¼ cup chopped celery

¼ cup chopped carrot

1 tablespoon all-purpose flour

2 14½-ounce cans chicken broth

1 5–6 ounce boneless, skinless chicken breast, cut into ½-inch cubes

2 ounces egg noodles

1. Melt the butter in a medium saucepan over medium heat. Add the onion, celery, and carrot, and cook for 5 minutes to soften. Sprinkle the flour into the pan and stir to blend. Add the broth and bring liquid to a boil. Reduce the heat to low and simmer for 5 minutes.

2. Add the cubed chicken and simmer 5 minutes longer. Add the egg noodles and simmer until the noodles are tender, about 10 minutes. Serve the soup hot.

Makes 4 servings

Chewing the Fat with Moe

● ● ● ● ● ● ● ● ● ● ● ● ● ●

Despite your best efforts, the recipes in this book may occasionally (OK, *frequently*) turn out to be tough, rubbery, and impossible to chew. This is not necessarily a bad thing. You just need to know how to chew like Moe.

Resilient foods are a challenge to Moe. Rather than discard a leathery meal, Moe intensifies his chewing until he has conquered and swallowed the enemy. Not even a piranha chews like Moe.

Clip and save this page for when the chewing gets tough. You never know when a chef like Curly will slip a potholder into a recipe in place of a pancake.

1. Become angry at tough and rubbery food.

2. Stab food homicidally with fork, bending fork in half.

3. Place food in mouth. Attempt to chew.

4. Grab chin with one hand and hair with the other hand.

5. Pull down on chin and up on hair until mouth is fully open.

6. Reverse motion until mouth closes. Repeat at furious pace until food is completely chewed.

7. While swallowing, thump yourself on the forehead several times to ensure smooth digestion.

Naki, Saki, and Waki's Jiu Jitsu Ginger Salad

Difficulty Level: Pussywillowbrain

Military historians still argue about the Stooges.

Some claim that Moe, Larry, and Curly were inadequate soldiers because they fell asleep on the battlefield, enraged superiors, and blew up their own admiral's battleship.

But others point to the day when the Stooges posed as Japanese soldiers Naki, Saki, and Waki, in order to gather intelligence behind enemy lines in *No Dough Boys*.

The mission was a nail-biter. Three beautiful enemy under-cover operatives, suspecting that the Stooges are imposters, challenge Naki, Saki, and Waki to demonstrate the ancient martial art of jiu jitsu. Not wanting to blow their cover, the Stooges jump, yelp, and fling each other across the room until it is clear that jiu jitsu is indeed a very strange art.

· ·

2 tablespoons orange juice

2 teaspoons white wine vinegar

3 tablespoons extra-virgin olive oil

½ teaspoon ground ginger

Salt and freshly ground black pepper to taste

2 quarts mixed salad greens, cleaned and torn

2 avocados, pitted, peeled, and sliced

2 navel oranges, peeled, separated into segments

1. Make a dressing by mixing the orange juice, vinegar, oil, and ginger together. Season it with salt and pepper.

2. In a large salad bowl, toss the greens with most of the dressing. Arrange the greens on serving plates. Top each salad with slices of avocado and orange segments. Drizzle salads with the remaining dressing.

Makes 4 servings

Naki, Saki, and Waki in *No Dough Boys*

A Bountiful Caesar Salad from the Great Lost Era of Mohicus, Larrycus, and Curlycue, Humble Servants to Octopus Grabus, Nearsighted Ruler of Ancient Erysipelas

Difficulty Level: Sap

Thousands of years after its golden age, little is known about ancient Erysipelas, site of the action in *Matri-Phony*.

Records do exist of three potters known as "The Biggest Chiselers in Town," but linguists remain baffled over the origin of the proprietors' names, Mohicus, Larrycus, and Curlycue. Surviving documents identify Octopus Grabus as ruler of the land, and make constant mention of his nearsightedness and inexplicable attraction to Curlycue.

No history of Erysipelian food survives. Researchers, however, suggest that Erysipelas might have influenced the development of Rome, with Octopus Grabus the model for a young Julius Caesar. To that end, this recipe for Caesar salad has been developed to honor this once great civilization.

··

2 quarts coarsely torn romaine lettuce leaves

5 tablespoons bottled Caesar dressing

Freshly ground black pepper to taste

1 cup garlic-flavored salad croutons

¼ cup grated Parmesan cheese

4 anchovy fillets, well drained

1. In a large salad bowl, toss the romaine with the dressing to coat the leaves evenly. Grind pepper over lettuce and toss again. Add the croutons and cheese. Toss well.

2. Divide the salad between two large serving plates. Arrange the anchovy fillets in a crisscross pattern atop each salad.

Makes 2 servings

Get yer fresh fish!

Hangover Athletic Club's Beer Belly Soup

Difficulty Level: Termite

The sport of wrestling has produced some legendary beer bellies, but none more majestic than the one belonging to Ivan Bustoff in *Grips, Grunts and Groans.*

The Stooges meet Bustoff in the rough-and-tumble Hangover Athletic Club, where they are supposed to keep an eye on the heavyweight until the big fight. But the wrestler's thirst for liquor pins him to the floor in nothing flat, a situation Bustoff's shady—and murderous—managers don't appreciate.

Had the Stooges fed him soup instead of spirits, Bustoff might still be wrestling today. Learn from Bustoff's mistake. Eat plenty of the Hangover Athletic Club's Beer Belly Soup and you'll expand your waist to championship proportions.

....

2 tablespoons butter or margarine

¼ cup frozen chopped onion

¼ cup frozen chopped green pepper

3 tablespoons flour

1 14½-ounce can chicken broth

1 12-ounce can beer

1½ cups shredded cheddar cheese

1. Melt the butter in a medium saucepan over medium–low heat. Add the onion and green pepper. Cook for 3 minutes to soften. Stir in the flour and cook another 2 minutes. Stir in the broth and beer. Bring the liquid to a boil, then reduce the heat to low and simmer for 10 minutes, stirring occasionally.

2. Stir in the shredded cheese. Heat only until the cheese melts. Serve immediately.

Makes 4 servings

Nice Soup from a Nice, Juicy Bone

Difficulty Level: Blubberhead

Gourmet cooking isn't cheap. Intricate delicacies like Roast Stooge (page 150) and Sloppy Moes (page 123) will fracture budgets faster than Larry can block a poke in the eye.

But don't despair if you're destitute. Instead, learn from Curly, who prepares Nice Soup from a Nice, Juicy Bone for just pennies a serving in *If a Body Meets a Body*. (Moe claims that the recipe tastes like a horse, but on a pauper's budget, is he expecting prime rib?)

> "We sent you to the butcher shop for meat, not to the glue factory."
>
> Moe, angry that he found a horseshoe in the soup Curly has prepared in *If a Body Meets a Body*

Stooges' Nice Soup from a Nice, Juicy Bone

1 horse (alive, but drowsy)

1 cauldron bubbling, boiling water

1 jumbo hammer

Approach drowsy horse cautiously. Use hammer to remove one of its shoes. Drop horseshoe into cauldron of bubbling, boiling water. Stir plaintively while contemplating your status as a pauper. Enjoy.

Another Nice Soup from a Nice, Juicy Bone:
Hearty Beef and Cabbage Soup

••

1 pound bone-in beef shank

1 tablespoon vegetable oil

1 large yellow onion, chopped

1 small head (1¼ pounds) green cabbage,
cored, sliced ½ inch thick

1 quart water

1 14½ ounce can diced tomatoes, drained

1 bay leaf

1 teaspoon salt

¼ teaspoon freshly ground black pepper

2 tablespoons apple cider vinegar

2 tablespoons brown sugar

Hot sauce to taste

6 tablespoons sour cream

1. In a large saucepan over medium–high heat, brown the beef shank in oil on both sides. Remove the shank to a cutting board. Reduce the heat to medium under pan and add the onion. Cook for 2 minutes and add the cabbage. Cook and stir until cabbage wilts, about 5 minutes. Add the water, diced tomatoes, and bay leaf. Bring the liquid to a boil.

2. Meanwhile, remove the meat from the shank bone and cut into bite-size pieces. Add the meat and the bone to the boiling liquid, then reduce the heat to low. Simmer, partially covered, for about 1½ hours until the meat is very tender. Remove the bone and the bay leaf from the soup. Stir in the salt and pepper.

3. In a small dish, mix the vinegar with the brown sugar. Add it to the soup and simmer for 10 minutes longer. Add hot sauce to taste.

4. Spoon hot soup into bowls and add a spoonful of sour cream to each. Serve immediately.

Makes 6 servings

"Swinging the Alphabet" Soup

Difficulty Level: Halibut

Generations of children have learned life's essential lessons from the Stooges.

Always block an eye poke. Don't waste a pie by eating it. Learn the alphabet through song and dance.

The Stooges sing "Swinging the Alphabet" for a college classroom in *Violent is the Word for Curly*, ensuring that university students will never again forget their ABCs. But the catchy little ditty is not strictly for educational use. Creative cooks rely on it to inspire fantastical alphabet soups. You should, too.

Stooges' "Swinging the Alphabet" Soup

• •

1 package alphabet soup letters
(heavy on the vowels)

1 pot boiling water

Contemplate how difficult life would be if you didn't know the alphabet. Open package of alphabet soup letters. Separate vowels from consonants. Begin to drop letters into boiling water while using your glorious soprano to sing "Swinging the Alphabet":

(To illustrate the letter B*)*

B—A—Bay
B—E—Bee
B—I—Bickee Bye
B—O—Boe
Bicky Bye Boe B—U—Boo
Bicky Bye Boe Boo!

(Note to readers still shaky with their ABCs: To learn the rest of the alphabet, make substitutions for the letter *B* above.)

Another "Swinging the Alphabet" Soup

••

1 14½-ounce can chicken broth

3 tablespoons water

1 small carrot, peeled, cut into thin rounds

2 tablespoons frozen tiny peas

1 ounce (about 3 tablespoons) alphabet-shaped
macaroni, or other tiny pasta shape

Grated Parmesan cheese to taste

1. Combine the broth and the water in a small saucepan and
bring liquid to a boil. Add the carrot rounds and frozen peas.
Reduce the heat to low, cover the pan, and cook until carrots
are tender, about 5 minutes.

2. Add the pasta and simmer the soup, uncovered, until pasta is
tender, 7 to 10 minutes. Sprinkle each serving of soup with
cheese, as desired.

Makes 2 servings

The Stooges on their way to "Swinging the Alphabet"
•••

Chapter 8

> **Moe:** Sit down and eat your dinner like a gentleman.
>
> **Shemp:** I'll eat, but I'll promise nothin'.
>
> *Pardon My Backfire*

We *all* added the yeast!

Dinner

Panther Pilsner Pie-Eyed Hot Dogs

Difficulty Level: Hot Airedale

This is the saddest of recipes.

There is barely a soul alive who isn't aware that Moe, Larry, and Curly went to prison for brewing their own refreshing Panther Pilsner Beer in *Beer Barrel Polecats*.

Few men loved beer and hot dogs more than the Stooges. Had nosy law enforcement officers minded their own business and not arrested the three bootleggers, it is certain that the Stooges would have created Panther Pilsner Pie-Eyed Hot Dogs. Since they never got that chance, it is the distinct honor of this cookbook to do it for them.

Stooges' Panther Pilsner Pie-Eyed Hot Dogs

1 can hops

1 can malt

1 canoe paddle

9 kegs yeast

1 burlap sack

1 rubber boot

1 bathtub

Mix hops and malt in a large crock. Fill with hot water and then merrily declare, "Hotsy totsy!" Add more hot water, but miss the crock and pour it down the collar of an irritable friend's shirt. Apologize by saying, "Take it easy, Moe; I'm a citizen!" Stir crock with canoe paddle.

Add 3 kegs yeast, then answer ringing phone in another room. Have a friend add 3 more kegs yeast without your knowledge. Have that friend answer another phone. Have third friend add 3 more kegs yeast without your knowledge. Allow mixture to boil over disastrously due to the extra yeast. Scoop up suds and dump them into burlap sack, rubber boot, and bathtub. Yields 1,000 bottles. Do not sell to police.

Bring beer to boil in rusty pot. Drop in hot dogs. Enjoy.

Another Panther Pilsner Pie-Eyed Hot Dogs

1 12-ounce can beer

1 cup drained sauerkraut

4 all-beef hot dogs

4 hot dog buns, warmed and split

Brown mustard

1. Combine the beer and sauerkraut in a saucepan over medium heat. Bring the mixture to a simmer; then add the hot dogs. Cover the pan and reduce the heat to low. Cook until hot dogs are heated through, about 5 minutes.

2. Put steamed hot dogs into the warm buns. Strain out the sauerkraut and place on top of the meat. Serve with brown mustard.

Makes 4 servings

Learning to duck is part of every good cook's repertoire.

Roast Stooge

Difficulty Level: Half-Wit

Imagine this nightmare. You are an innocent tree surgeon and travel to the exotic island of Rhum Boogie in search of the rare Puckerless Persimmon tree. Your motives are pure, but vicious island savages determine to cook you for dinner, and even list you on their evening supper menu.

Something from an episode of the *Twilight Zone*? Hardly. This terrible incident actually happens to the Stooges in *Some More of Samoa*.

The terror peaks when natives stuff an apple into Curly's mouth, measure his ribs and calf for steaks, then prepare a boiling cauldron into which he and select vegetables are to be dropped.

"I personally brought you your last meal before you are shot. Eat hearty! Pigs feet smothered in lubricating oil, raw potatoes boiled in pure varnish, and head cheese garnished with nails . . . rusty nails!"

Anemian official to the Stooges in *Hot Stuff*

The tribal chief's daughter offers Curly his freedom if he agrees to marry her, but in the greatest demonstration of bravery in Stooge history, Curly takes one look at her homely mug and decides that he prefers to be boiled alive.

Curly does try to reason with the natives, arguing, "You can't eat me, I'm too tough. I'll give you indigestion!" They are not persuaded.

It is every Stooge fan's good fortune that Moe, Larry, and Curly were masters of escape; otherwise, the Rhum Boogians would have been the last to enjoy them. But that doesn't mean cooks cannot prepare a noncannibal version of Roast Stooge. Just remember not to drop a friend into the pot; humans are too tough and they give you indigestion.

Brisket

••

1 brisket (up to 10 pounds; increase gravy and
onions for more meat)

1 medium yellow onion, sliced

Vegetable oil

Seasoned salt to taste

Freshly ground black pepper to taste

Garlic powder to taste

Ketchup

1½ cups black coffee

2 tablespoons Kitchen Bouquet
(or any other gravy maker)

1. Dry the brisket with paper towels. In a large frying pan over
medium heat, brown onion in oil. Place brisket fat-side down
in frying pan. Brown for 5 minutes. Turn meat over and season top (fat side) generously (or to taste) with seasoned salt,
pepper, and garlic powder. Spread approximately 2 tablespoons ketchup on meat. Brown five more minutes.

2. Preheat oven to 375°F.

3. Turn meat, then season other side with seasoned salt, pepper,
and garlic. Spread ketchup.

4. Place meat fat-side up with onions in roaster and place in the
oven. Make gravy by mixing coffee, Kitchen Bouquet, and 7
tablespoons ketchup in a small bowl. Poke the meat several
times with a fork and pour the gravy over it. Cover and cook
for 1½ hours or until meat is browned throughout. After each
½ hour of cooking, remove and baste meat. To serve, cut
meat into ¼-inch slices against the grain.

Makes 6–8 servings

No newspaper ever reviewed a Stooges restaurant. Had such a review been written, it might have looked like this:

The Flounder Inn

●●●●●●●●●●●●●●●

By Maximillian Sniffington,
Food Critic
(Based on scenes from the film
Playing the Ponies)

Opened by three rather unusual gentlemen, the Flounder Inn is the latest neighborhood seafood establishment. Two days after visiting, however, I can say with confidence that this was the most unsettling dining I have experienced in 25 years as a critic.

While waiting to be seated, I observed one of the proprietors, a bushy-haired man apparently known as Larry, ringing up a customer's tab at the cash register. He properly asked after the quality of the food, to which the patron growled, "The soup was watery, the steak was tough, and the coffee was just like mud!" Bafflingly, this man Larry replied only by saying, "Well, I'm glad you liked it. Don't forget to tell your friends."

Perhaps this strange interchange should have provided a glimpse of things to come, but my stomach was empty and the daily special—Lobster with Frog Legs—was mouthwateringly priced at 35 cents. I decided to forget the odd cash register incident and sat down to enjoy my meal.

It took only a moment for a stern-looking waiter by the name of Moe to arrive at my table. I promptly ordered the special but was informed that it was no longer available. Disappointed, I ordered a hot dog. Rather than write my order on a proper waiter's tablet, this man had the insolence to yell to the kitchen, "One bow-wow!" I was appalled at such rude service, but was even more devastated to see a bald and rotund chef respond to the order by chasing a dog from the kitchen with a meat cleaver!

Naturally, I changed my order to eggs on toast. Again the waiter bellowed to the kitchen, this time calling for "Adam and Eve on a raft!" When I instructed him to scramble the eggs, he cried, "Wreck 'em!"

Lest you think this unsettling lack of decorum to be an isolated incident, I can attest to similar disturbances at tables nearby. One distressed customer asked this same waiter, Moe, whether the dish he had been served was pork or veal. The waiter asked, "What did you order?" to which the customer replied, "Veal." Shockingly, the waiter snapped, "Then it's veal!"

Another patron, who seemed on the verge of a nervous breakdown, asked the waiter why a dog had run up to his table and started growling. "Oh, don't mind him," the waiter replied casually. "He's mad because you're eating out of his plate."

Noise and commotion at the Flounder Inn exceeded acceptable levels. On more than one occasion, I witnessed the host and waiter charging recklessly through the swinging doors leading into the kitchen, injuring the unsuspecting party on the other side. When I complained about such behavior, waiter Moe could only mutter this insufficient apology: "I'm at a loss for adjectives."

The restaurant does incorporate an ingenious billing method. As a customer approached the cash register, the bushy-haired chap grabbed his necktie, peered at the stains closely and remarked, "Lemme see . . . you had chicken soup, tenderloin steak, and coffee." When one dishonest customer tried to leave, Larry pulled his tie back and scolded, "Uh-uh, custard pie!"

Sadly, I cannot recommend the Flounder Inn. The food was putrid and the service suspect. Even the fish—the restaurant's specialty—was tough and inedible. (The filet of sole tasted suspiciously like a rubber boot, and might more appropriately be dubbed Filet of Sole and Heel.) The only positive is the chili pepperinos available for free at the cash register; they pack a mighty wallop and could turn even a nag of a racehorse into Man O' War.

Sniffington's Rating: 0 stars

This customer at the Flounder Inn thinks the soup is watery, the steak is tough, and the coffee is muddy. Maybe he'd like a mint?

Fillet of Sole and Heel

Difficulty Level: Lamebrain

Finicky customers at the Stooge-owned Flounder Inn complain that the soup is watery, the steak tough, and the coffee muddy. Perfectionists.

But patrons savvy enough to order seafood from the Flounder Inn's kitchen are richly rewarded. The Lobster with Frog Legs (competitively priced at 35 cents) is heavenly, but nothing compares to Chef Curly's masterpiece, Fillet of Sole and Heel.

Perhaps it is his choice of exotic ingredients (not every cook is bold enough to call for a rubber boot in his recipes), or perhaps it is his instinct for seasonings (only flour is added for flavor). Whatever his secrets, it is safe to say that Chef Curly's frying pan is a place of honor for any fish lucky enough to be chosen for the next serving of the famous Fillet of Sole and Heel.

> "What do you think I am, a lobster?"
>
> Moe, after Larry tries to loosen glue stuck to Moe's lips by splashing boiling water on his face in *Healthy, Wealthy and Dumb*

Stooges' Fillet of Sole and Heel

1 fishing pole

12 cups flour

1 cleaver

1 frying pan

Open the window nearest to the kitchen. Use fishing pole to cast a line out the window and into nearest stream, river, lake, or ocean. Catch a black rubber boot (knee-length or longer), and allow the boot to pull you violently into the window frame as if you'd hooked a whale. Reel in the boot. Briefly celebrate your catch by declaring, "Oh, boy!" Use cleaver to chop heel off boot. Smother heel in flour, then drop boot into a sizzling frying pan. Sing "La-lee, la-la-lee" for 10 seconds until boot is done.

Moe (holding a barking fish): Look what we got for breakfast.

Shemp: Oh, boy, a dogfish!

Larry: I hope it ain't got fleas!

I'm a Monkey's Uncle

Another Fillet of Sole and Heel: Broiled Whitefish

2 tablespoons butter, melted

1 teaspoon lemon juice

¼ teaspoon paprika

2 6–8 ounce whitefish fillets

Vegetable oil

Salt and freshly ground black pepper to taste

Lemon wedges and tartar sauce, as needed

1. Preheat oven broiler. In a small dish, mix the melted butter with the lemon juice and paprika.

2. Rub the skin of the fillets lightly with vegetable oil, and place them on a baking sheet, oiled-side down. Brush the fillets with the butter mixture, and sprinkle with salt and pepper. Place the pan under the broiler about 4 inches from the heat source. Broil until the fish is done, about 7 minutes.

3. Serve whitefish with lemon wedges and tartar sauce.

Makes 2 servings

"We've been trying to sell these fish for 30 days and haven't got rid of one."

Moe, assessing the recent performance of the Stooges' fish business in *Cookoo Cavaliers*

How I Shall Gobble This Gobbler!

Difficulty Level: Skillethead

The history books don't say so, but the Pilgrims invented Thanksgiving for chefs like Curly.

No one prepares stuffed turkey like Curly. From his avant-garde approach to stuffing to the actual capture of the turkey itself, Curly works wonders with this festive bird that would leave John Smith and Pocahontas speechless.

Stooges' How I Shall Gobble This Gobbler!

....

1 musket (Revolutionary War vintage, if possible)

2 eggs

2 potatoes

Pinch of salt

6 oysters

1 can green peas

1 loaf of bread (well soaked)

1 zipper

1 pair pliers

1 bathroom plunger

1 gigantic pair scissors

Take musket to a deserted field, then fire the weapon directly overhead. Wait gleefully with arms outstretched until a turkey falls from the sky. Declare joyously, like Curley, "How I shall gobble this gobbler!" Return to kitchen.

Place turkey on large cutting board, pound on its chest and declare it to be musclebound. Test its structural integrity by furiously flapping its wings, then use pliers to clip any hang-nails you find on the bird.

Separate two eggs by moving each egg to an opposite side of the cutting board. Then drop them into the turkey without removing the shells.

Dice two potatoes by shaking them like casino dice and then roll into turkey. Measure a pinch of salt by vigorously pinching it from a container and then throw inside the turkey.

Gather six oysters, inspect one, and declare, "Oh, they forgot to clean this one!" Remove and discard the meat from the oysters and place the shells inside the turkey.

Stuff the can of peas into the turkey. If a meddlesome associate like Moe comes along and scolds you for failing to remove the paper label from the can of peas, defer to his judgment and remove the label; then stuff can back into turkey.

Hold loaf of bread firmly in one hand; then soak it well by pummeling with your fists. Insert into turkey with the aid of bathroom plunger.

Secure stuffing contents by zipping the turkey's zipper.

Cook at 650°F until turkey is burned to a blackened crisp. Remove bird from oven and place scalding pan onto the back of a nearby friend who happens to be bending over.

Carve the bird using a jumbo pair of scissors, being careful not to notice the lengthy beards of dinner guests, which should be carved off as well. Serve.

Moe: Our first move is to kick the stuffing out of turkey!
Larry (lifting dinner roll): I'll wipe out grease!
I'll Never Heil Again

Another How I Shall Gobble This Gobbler: Stuffed Turkey

· ·

¼ cup (½ stick) butter or margarine, melted,
plus 2 tablespoons softened

1½ cups chopped onion

1 cup chopped celery

1 teaspoon dried sage

1 teaspoon dried thyme

1 teaspoon celery seeds

½ teaspoon salt, plus extra for seasoning bird

12 ounces bread cubes for stuffing

¼ teaspoon freshly ground black pepper,
plus extra for seasoning bird

¾ cup canned chicken broth

Whole turkey (10–12 pounds), neck and giblets
removed, rinsed and patted dry

1. To make the bread stuffing, pour 2 tablespoons of the melted butter into a medium skillet over medium heat. Add the onion, celery, sage, thyme, celery seeds, and ½ teaspoon of the salt. Cover the pan and cook until onion and celery are soft, 5 to 7 minutes.

2. Pour the contents of the skillet into a large bowl. Add the bread cubes and toss the mixture together. Season it with ¼ teaspoon of the pepper. Drizzle on the remaining 2 tablespoons melted butter. Add the broth and toss to moisten the bread cubes evenly.

3. Preheat an oven to 350°F. Season the turkey cavity lightly with salt and pepper. Stuff the turkey with as much of the bread stuffing as fits, without packing it. Put any remaining stuffing into a baking dish to bake separately. Fold the wings of the bird backward to secure the neck flap in place. If the metal clasp is missing, tie drumsticks together. Rub the turkey skin with the softened butter and season it with salt and pepper.

4. Place the stuffed turkey on a rack in a roasting pan and set into the oven. After 2 hours, or when the bird is golden brown, tent aluminum foil loosely over the skin. Continue to roast until done, allowing 3 to 3½ hours of total oven time. Turn the turkey out onto a cutting board, tent with foil, and let it cool 30 minutes before carving.

Makes 10 to 12 servings

Why go to the grocery when you can get it fresh?

Ivan Bustoff's Barrel-Chested Beef Stew

Difficulty Level: Musclebrain

In boxing's glory days, fighters built muscle not with steroids or in the weight room, but by ingesting mountains of steaks and rivers of beer. This diet didn't do much to sculpt their physiques, but it turned the beer belly and barrel chest into lethal weapons.

No wonder wrestler Ivan Bustoff was the deadliest wrestler of his day. Just look at the bountiful belly and chest he throws around in *Grips, Grunts and Groans*. Even Curly, whose upper dimensions are nothing to sneeze at, fails to hold a candle to Bustoff in the ring.

Health nuts may yap forever about the benefits of eating sprouts and hay. True tough guys know that there's nothing like a good beef stew for building a silo-sized torso. Lift weights if you wish; even hire a personal trainer. But remember that consuming several helpings of Ivan Bustoff's Barrel-Chested Beef Stew is the only real way for a champion to get his start in the ring.

· ·

½ cup flour

1 teaspoon salt

½ teaspoon freshly ground black pepper

2 pounds beef stew meat

¼ cup bacon fat or lard

¼ cup bourbon

2 medium onions, chopped coarse

1 bay leaf

½ teaspoon dried thyme

2 14½-ounce cans beef broth

¼ cup steak sauce

1 pound frozen assorted vegetables for stew,
thawed and drained

1. Mix the flour, salt, and pepper together in a bowl. Toss the meat into the seasoned flour to coat well. Shake off excess flour, and set aside on a tray. Melt the fat over medium–high heat in a dutch oven.

2. While the fat is getting hot, dredge the meat in the flour mixture a second time. Brown the floured meat in batches. Be careful not to overcrowd the pan. Set the meat aside. Stir the bourbon into the pan drippings, then add the onions, bay leaf, and thyme. Return all browned meat to the pan.

3. Pour in the broth and bring the liquid to a boil. Stir in the steak sauce, cover the pan, and reduce the heat to low. Simmer the stew about 1½ hours, stirring occasionally, until the meat is tender. Add the assorted vegetables to the stew and simmer until the vegetables are hot and cooked through.

4. Serve beef stew with boiled potatoes.

Makes 6 servings

Learning to use chopsticks

Cousin Basil's Knockout Basil Chicken

Difficulty Level: Chowderhead

Shemp is about to strike it rich in *Brideless Groom*. His uncle Caleb has passed away and left him $500,000 . . . provided Shemp gets married by 6 P.M.

Uncle Caleb was a dear man, Shemp says, the kind of guy "who'd give you the shirt off his back and throw in the buttons, too." But he overestimated Shemp's appeal to women. After proposing to and being rejected by every lady in his little black book, it appears that Shemp will stay single—and broke—forever.

But there seems to be hope yet. A stunning blond has just moved in down the hall. Even better, she's single.

Shemp shaves. Shemp applies cologne. Shemp heeds Moe's order to "get sexy."

The plan works like a charm . . . for a while. Believing Shemp to be her beloved cousin Basil, the blond showers him with a lifetime supply of ear-popping smooches and cuddly bear hugs. Eavesdropping outside the apartment door, Moe and Larry are convinced that the blond has fallen hopelessly in love with Shemp. Moe is so happy he gives Larry a big kiss for good measure.

> "Now, Penelope, I expect a blessed event by morning: a nice, big, fat fryer with giblets and gravy!"
>
> Curly, to a barnyard hen from whom he desires eggs in *The Yoke's on Me*

But when the actual cousin Basil phones the blond, her opinion of Shemp changes. Drastically. Several slaps and a devastating right cross later, Shemp is no closer to marriage than he was before being mistaken for cousin Basil.

Thank goodness for true love. Miss Dinkelmeyer, Shemp's singing student, wanted to marry him all along. Shemp was just too disoriented by her off-kilter warbling to have noticed. It is not known what Shemp and Miss Dinkelmeyer ate to celebrate their marriage, but a serving of Cousin Basil's Knockout Basil Chicken would have been the perfect romantic touch.

··

4 boneless, skinless chicken breast halves

Salt and freshly ground black pepper to taste

1½ tablespoons butter

2 tablespoons minced green onion

2 tablespoons dry vermouth

1 cup diced tomatoes

1 cup canned chicken broth

½ cup heavy cream

6 large fresh basil leaves, shredded

1. Season the chicken with salt and pepper. Heat the butter in a skillet over medium heat and brown the breasts 2 minutes on each side. Remove the chicken to a plate and discard excess butter from the pan.

2. Add the onion, vermouth, tomatoes, and chicken broth to the skillet. Cook briskly 3 to 4 minutes to reduce liquid slightly. Add the cream and return the chicken to the pan. Simmer until the meat is thoroughly cooked, about 5 minutes, turning once. Sprinkle with the basil and season the sauce with salt and pepper, if necessary. Serve immediately.

Makes 4 servings

Larry's Chicken in a Bag

Difficulty Level: Buttonhead

With a recipe like this in his repertoire, it's a miracle Larry became a Stooge rather than a chef. Chicken in a Bag—a dish as dramatic and creative as Larry's own hairstyle—was one of his favorites; it appears here courtesy of his grand-daughter, Kris Cutler.

1 teaspoon flour

1 large cooking bag

10 carrots, peeled and sliced thick

8 stalks celery, sliced thick

1 medium onion, cut into wedges

6 medium red or white potatoes, cut in half

Salt to taste

Freshly ground black pepper to taste

Paprika to taste

8 pieces chicken (washed and dried)

1. Preheat oven to 350°F.

2. Place flour into cooking bag and shake to coat. Put carrots, celery, onion, and potatoes in the bag. Add salt, pepper, and paprika to taste.

3. Place chicken in bag on top of vegetables. Tie bag closed and make six slits in the top.

4. Bake for one hour.

5. Remove the bag from the oven and cut it open. Pour chicken and vegetables onto plate, covering with juices.

"Boy, could I tear that chicken to smithereenees!"

Moe, *Half Shot Shooters*

Moe and Larry teach Joe to use better table manners.

Honest Moe, Honest Shemp and . . . Larry's Rickety Chariot Wheel Pasta

Difficulty Level: Birdbrain

During the reign of the great King Rootentooten in *Mummy's Dummies*, there was only one place to shop for a used chariot: the Smiling Egyptians.

Manned by the legendary sales force of Honest Moe, Honest Shemp and . . . Larry, the Smiling Egyptians guaranteed value for your shekels. Unless your salesman happened to be Larry.

None of the Stooges, actually, was blameless for selling a lemon of a chariot to Radames, the sourpuss chief of King Rootentooten's palace guard. Had even a single feature on the chariot worked as advertised, Radames might not have demanded the death penalty for the Stooges.

Now that men drive cars instead of chariots, are there any lessons to be learned from the questionable practices of the Smiling Egyptians? The answer is no. But you can enjoy the wagon wheel pasta dish that was inspired by their exploits. Just don't overcook the pasta; that makes the wagon wheels as rickety as those that fell off Radames's chariot.

· ·

12 ounces mild or hot Italian sausage

2 tablespoons olive oil

2 small green bell peppers, cored, seeded,
cut into ½-inch chunks

1 small yellow onion, cut into ½-inch chunks

2 garlic cloves, chopped

1 tablespoon chopped fresh oregano

1 14½-ounce can diced tomatoes, drained

½ teaspoon salt

¼ teaspoon freshly ground black pepper

12 ounces wagon wheel pasta

Parmesan cheese (optional)

1. Cut the sausage into ½-inch slices. Cook in a medium skillet over medium heat, turning to brown all over. Remove browned meat and set aside.

2. Add the oil to the skillet, and when hot, add the peppers and onion. Cook and stir until softened and lightly colored, about 10 minutes. Add the garlic, oregano, tomatoes, and the browned sausage meat. Season with the salt and pepper. Cover the pan and cook over low heat for 8 to 10 minutes until sausage and peppers are thoroughly cooked.

3. Meanwhile, cook the pasta in a large pot of boiling salted water according to package directions. Drain the pasta and toss with the sauce.

4. Sprinkle each serving of pasta with grated Parmesan cheese, if desired.

Makes 4 servings

The Stooges never cook without fair warning.

Howard's End

Difficulty Level: Nesthead

Thank goodness for the hind quarters. Without his, Curly would not have lasted long.

Curly doesn't rely on stuntmen, choosing instead to dampen the many kicks he takes from Moe the natural way, with his ample rear end. As a bonus, his two hind cheeks always compensate for his two left feet on the dance floor.

Few cooks choose to think about such matters while cooking, yet it would be a grave oversight to exclude a recipe that honored Curly's posterior. Howard's End—a delicious rump roast—should provide the perfect balance between good taste and good taste.

Rump Pot Roast

••

2 pounds boneless tied rump roast

1 tablespoon lard or other shortening

1 small yellow onion, chopped fine

Salt and freshly ground black pepper to taste

⅔ cup water

2 medium potatoes, peeled, quartered

2 large carrots, peeled, quartered

4 celery stalks, quartered

2 teaspoons beef-flavored bouillon granules

2 tablespoons all-purpose flour

2½ cups hot water

1. Preheat oven to 350°F.

2. In a Dutch oven over medium–high heat, brown the beef in the lard on all sides. Remove the meat from the pan and add the onion. Cook and stir until slightly softened, about 3 minutes. Return the meat to the pan and season it with salt and pepper. Add ⅔ cup water, cover the pan tightly, and set into the conventional oven. Bake for 2 hours. Liquid should nearly evaporate during baking.

3. Uncover the roast and add the potatoes, carrots, and celery. Dissolve 1 teaspoon of the bouillon granules in 1 cup of hot water, and add it to the beef and vegetables. Re-cover the pan and return it to the oven. Bake 1 hour longer, until meat and vegetables are tender.

4. Remove the meat and set aside on a cutting board, tented with aluminum foil. Place the cooked potatoes, carrots, and celery on a platter and keep warm. To make a pan gravy, sprinkle the flour into the roasting juices and stir to blend.

> "I'm just crazy about Spanish food, especially corned beef and cabbage!"
>
> Curly, *Three Sappy People*

5. Dissolve the remaining teaspoon of bouillon granules in 1½ cups hot water, and stir it into the flour mixture. Bring to a simmer over medium heat. Cook and stir until the gravy thickens, 2 to 3 minutes. Adjust the seasoning with salt and pepper.

6. Carve the roast into thick slices and serve with the cooked vegetables and pan gravy.

Makes 4 servings

Curly Joe's Favorite Roast Beef

Difficulty Level: Squirrelbait

No Stooge was beefier than Curly Joe, so it is with extreme pleasure that his personal roast beef recipe is presented to hungry Stooge fans everywhere. (Jean DeRita, Curly Joe's wife, says that he liked to sprinkle garlic over the roast. You may, too, if you have a forgiving family.)

• •

1 small tritip roast

1 can mushroom soup

4 carrots, peeled and quartered

2 small potatoes, halved

½ package onion soup mix

powdered garlic (optional)

1. Place roast onto large piece of aluminum foil and then place into roasting pan.

2. In a small bowl, mix mushroom soup and a can of water; then pour mixture onto roast. Add carrots, potatoes, and onion soup mix. Add garlic powder if desired.

3. Wrap aluminum foil over roast and bake at 350°F for 1½ hours.

Moe's Anatomy of a Cow (and That Ain't No Bull)

● ● ● ● ● ● ● ● ● ● ● ● ● ●

The Stooges will strike it rich in *Busy Buddies* . . . if Curly can win the Carrot County Fair Champion Milking Contest.

Problem is, Curly has no idea how to operate a cow.

Moe never allows education to interfere with plans. Thinking quickly, he fashions a simple diagram of a cow to illustrate how the animal is put together. Curly loses, anyway.

But that doesn't mean such valuable information should be wasted. If you still believe a cow to be divided into T-bones, porterhouses, and chuck, memorize this list and use it the next time you dine out. Your waiter will be astonished.

According to Moe's diagram in *Busy Buddies*, a cow is composed of the following parts:

Auto Club Steaks (meats every Thursday)

Chopped liver

Corn beef

Filet of Sole and Heel

Franks

Hamburger

Hash

Hot dogs

Meat loaf

Meatballs

Salami

Spare ribs

Suki yaki

Weiner schnitzel

Wieners

Curly's Wish: Roast Chicken and Dumplings

Difficulty Level: Snoring Hyena

Something wonderful happens to Curly in *Oily to Bed, Oily to Rise*: his every wish comes true.

Blessed with such a talent, many of us might wish for a million dollars. Others might fancy diamonds or exotic cars.

Being a food lover, however, Curly wishes for roast chicken and dumplings. And some hot apple pie.

Sure enough, the Stooges arrive at the doorstep of a kindly old woman. She is the widow Jenkins, and she never turns away a hungry man . . . especially when she's whipping up roast chicken and dumplings. And some hot apple pie.

Best of all, the widow Jenkins has three beautiful daughters, April, May, and June, whom the Stooges marry after Curly successfully wishes for a justice of the peace. Follow the recipe below and you, too, can have roast chicken and dumplings. April, May, and June, however, are three dishes that forever belong to the Stooges.

· ·

3½-pound whole chicken, rinsed and patted dry

Salt and freshly ground black pepper to taste

Vegetable oil

2 cups self-rising flour

¼ cup finely chopped parsley

¼ cup (½ stick) cold margarine or shortening, cut into pieces

1 cup milk

2 14½-ounce cans chicken broth

1. Preheat oven to 400°F. Season the chicken cavity lightly with salt and pepper. Rub the outside skin with vegetable oil and sprinkle with salt and pepper. Place the chicken on a rack in a roasting pan and set into the oven to cook for 1 hour.

2. Meanwhile, prepare the dumplings. Combine the self-rising flour and parsley in a mixing bowl. Add the margarine pieces, cutting them into the flour using a fork until mixture is crumbly. Add the milk and mix to form a dough.

3. Heat the broth in a saucepan and bring it to a simmer. Drop the dumpling dough into simmering broth by rounded tablespoonfuls. Simmer them in the pan, uncovered, for 10 minutes. Cover the pan and simmer the dumplings 10 minutes longer.

4. Turn the roasted chicken onto a cutting board and carve into serving pieces. Place the chicken on serving plates with poached dumplings and some of the cooking broth.

Makes 6 servings

The widow Jenkins knows that the way to Curly's heart is through his stomach.

I. Fleecem's Lamb Chops

Difficulty Level: Clumsy Idiot

Arguably the most corrupt attorney ever to worm his way into the American Bar, I. Fleecem's handling of Shemp's estate in *Heavenly Daze* and *Bedlam in Paradise* is a case study in legal malpractice. And as president of Skin and Flint Finance Corporation in *Sing a Song of Six Pants* and *Rip, Sew and Stich*, Fleecem is only too ready to foreclose on Pip Boys, the Stooges' trend-setting but unprofitable tailor shop.

A sourpuss of a man like Fleecem is obviously in need of a warm, home-cooked meal. But what do you prepare for a man with such an ominous name? Lamb chops, naturally. Try this recipe and you'll see: even the shadiest lawyer will swear an oath to the honest goodness of I. Fleecem's Lamb Chops.

Moe: Pardon me. Are you going to eat that lamb alone?

Larry: No, I'll wait. Maybe I'll get something else!

Moe: Say, tell me, do you like asparagus?

Larry: Love 'em!

Moe (poking Larry's eyes): Well, here's a couple of tips for you!

Pardon My Backfire

"Hot stake is better than a cold chop."

Curly, explaining why he chooses to be executed by burning rather than by the axe in *Three Little Pirates*

· ·

Vegetable oil

4 lamb loin chops, 1 inch thick

Salt and freshly ground black pepper to taste

1. Preheat oven to 350°F. Place a cast-iron skillet over medium–high heat and coat the bottom of the pan with a film of vegetable oil. Sprinkle the chops with salt and pepper.

2. When the skillet is hot, brown the chops for 2 minutes on each side. Transfer the skillet to the oven, and bake the chops for 5 to 6 minutes or until the meat springs back when poked with a finger. Drain the chops of pan grease before serving.

3. Serve lamb chops with mint jelly, if desired.

Makes 2 servings

When preparing seafood, use only mild-mannered lobsters.

Aggie, Maggie, and Baggie's Thinly Veiled Veal Parmesan

Difficulty Level: Ironhead

Blind dates are risky business. Just look what happens to Shemp in *I'm a Monkey's Uncle*.

Dateless for the evening, caveman Shemp is delighted when caveman Moe agrees to fix up Larry and him with his girlfriend Aggie's sisters.

The date begins splendidly. "I'm Aggie," says Moe's girl-friend, a gorgeous specimen of a cavewoman who makes Moe swoon. "I'm Maggie," says Larry's date for the evening, a shapely goddess who sends shivers down Larry's spine.

Shemp can hardly wait as his blond and veiled cave-woman bats her eyelashes. "I'm Baggie," she says, removing her veil to reveal the mug of a mastodon. "You're telling me!" cries Shemp, suddenly content in his bachelorhood and cer-tain that blind dates are indeed a risky business.

"There you are, sir. You look very pretty, and the spaghetti is as good as new!"

Shemp, after using a scissors to cut a perfect sugar-bowl haircut from the spaghetti he spilled onto the head of a restaurant patron in *Rumpus in a Harem*

8 ounces veal scallopini

1 egg, beaten

⅓ cup dry bread crumbs

2 tablespoons butter

¾ cup marinara or pasta sauce

3 ounces sliced mozzarella cheese

3 tablespoons grated Parmesan cheese

1. Preheat oven to 350°F. Dip the veal into the beaten egg to coat it completely, then dredge the meat in the bread crumbs, shaking off excess crumbs.

2. Heat the butter in a skillet over medium heat, and when melted, add the breaded veal. Brown the meat 2 to 3 minutes on each side; then remove the meat from the skillet.

3. Spread half of the marinara sauce in the bottom of a baking dish large enough to fit the veal in a single layer. Arrange the veal pieces over the sauce. Place the mozzarella slices over the meat and spread the remaining sauce over the cheese. Sprinkle evenly with the Parmesan cheese. Bake in the oven until the cheese melts, about 15 minutes. Serve immediately.

Makes 2 servings

> ## I smell something burning . . . somebody's roasting a ham!
> Shemp, sitting on a scalding iron in *Hugs and Mugs*

Shemp's Stringy-Haired Spaghetti

Difficulty Level: Scissorbill

Had he pursued cooking, Shemp might have been a world-class chef. His fried eggs and stuffed turkey are still copied by culinary institutes today.

But Shemp faces obstacles never imagined by ordinary chefs. He is a poor speller, mistaking soap for soup and gloves for cloves. He is too often rough with ingredients, as when he pinches salt when the recipe calls for a pinch of salt, or pummels a loaf of bread when the recipe calls for a well-soaked loaf of bread. Most problematic, Moe doesn't like Shemp's cooking, and is not afraid to express that sentiment in painful ways.

Shemp's biggest cooking hurdle, however, is his hair. Long and stringy in front, it constantly swoops into his field of vision and causes temporary blindness. Without the ability to see, not even Shemp can cook effectively. This, more than any other factor, explains why Shemp became a Stooge rather than a chef.

This recipe recalls one of history's great chefs and the hairdo that made him great. Prepare it—using no hairnet—and serve with a loaf of fine French bread . . . well soaked.

Larry (bossy): Give the kid back his spaghetti; what're you gonna do, eat it yourself?

Moe (throwing pasta into Larry's face): No, you eat it.

Sock-A-Bye Baby

••

2 small zucchini, sliced thin

2 garlic cloves, chopped

2 tablespoons olive oil

Salt and freshly ground black pepper to taste

6 ounces dry angel hair pasta (capellini)

2 tablespoons butter

Grated rind or zest of 1 lemon

2 tablespoons fresh lemon juice

Grated Romano or Parmesan cheese, as needed

1. In a pan over medium heat, cook the zucchini and garlic in the olive oil, stirring, until zucchini softens and begins to brown, about 5 minutes. Season the zucchini with salt and pepper.

2. Meanwhile, cook the pasta in a large pot of boiling salted water according to package directions. Place the butter, lemon rind, and lemon juice into a large bowl. Spoon out 2 tablespoons of the pasta cooking water and add it to the bowl before draining the cooked pasta. Add the hot, drained pasta and cooked zucchini to the bowl and toss it all together.

3. Serve in pasta bowls with a generous sprinkling of grated cheese.

Makes 2 servings

Shemp (inspecting a turkey that's on fire and blackened to a crisp): I can't understand what happened to that turkey. I only had the dial set at 650 degrees.

Moe: Listen, if the cake in that oven turns out like this, you're going to be the next one to broil in it. And I'm going to baste you with nitric acid. Go on, fix that punch and make it snappy!

Shemp: But the lady said she wanted it weak!

Listen, Judge

Haunted Turkey

Difficulty Level: Bunionhead

Every chef knows the feeling.

You cook a chicken or a turkey, begin to carve it, and the bird lets out a bloodcurdling squawk and walks away.

Cooks should never blame themselves for these unfortunate incidents. Fowl have a great will to live.

Instead, try turning the oven up to 950°F. That won't necessarily kill the bird, but it should discourage it from making such a fuss during the carving phase.

Stooges' Haunted Turkey

· ·

1 fat turkey

1 package crackers

1 mischievous pet parrot

Cook fat turkey until golden brown. Become distracted by the foolishness of a nearby friend. While distracted, mischievous pet parrot will climb inside turkey.

Test sharpness of carving knife by painfully plucking hair from friend's head, then slicing it with knife. Try to stuff turkey with crackers, but become mystified as the turkey steals the crackers from your fingers.

Stab turkey with carving fork, then leap backward in horror as turkey emits a horrible yelp, jumps off the table, and begins walking around the kitchen. Begin weeping, and declare to everyone in the room that the turkey is haunted.

Catch the turkey and place it back on the table. Soothingly pet the bird in an effort to calm it into submission. When the turkey laughs uproariously, run out of the kitchen and do not return.

Another Haunted Turkey: Turkey Tetrazzini

¼ cup (½ stick) butter or margarine,
plus extra for topping

⅓ cup flour

2½ cups canned or homemade
chicken or turkey broth

2 cups half-and-half

3 tablespoons sherry

1 teaspoon salt, or more to taste

⅛ teaspoon ground white pepper

⅛ teaspoon ground nutmeg

1 pound dry spaghetti

1 quart cooked, boneless turkey chunks

1 cup cooked sliced mushrooms

½ cup dry bread crumbs

½ cup grated Parmesan cheese

1. To make a tetrazzini sauce, melt ¼ cup of the butter in a saucepan over medium–low heat. Add the flour and stir to blend. Cook and stir for 1 minute. Add the broth. Stir in the half-and-half, sherry, salt, pepper, and nutmeg. Simmer the sauce until just slightly thickened, about 10 minutes. Set the sauce aside to cool.

2. Preheat oven to 350°F. While the oven heats, cook the pasta in a large pot of boiling salted water according to package directions. Drain the pasta and place it in a large bowl.

3. Add the sauce to the pasta and stir to blend. Add the turkey and mushrooms and toss it all together. Pour the mixture into a greased 3-quart baking dish. Mix the bread crumbs and cheese together and sprinkle over the pasta. Dot the crumb topping with pieces of extra butter and set the dish into the oven to bake until bubbling hot, 30 to 35 minutes.

Makes 8 servings

Chapter 9

"Have this refilled!"

Curly, handing a banana peel to
B. O. Davis in *So Long, Mr. Chumps*

Desserts

Sword of Damocles Triple Cream Pie

Difficulty Level: Slug

God works in mysterious ways. To some He gives power, to others prestige. To the Stooges, He gives cream pies.

In Stooge hands, the cream pie becomes more than dessert; it becomes the great equalizer.

Observe the snootiness at fancy parties attended by the Stooges. Invariably, blue-blooded guests turn their noses up when the Stooges enter the room, as if their finishing school demeanors are any more worthy than the Stooges' slightly less polished comportment.

Snobs.

The Stooges, to their credit, don't take such slights sitting down. Especially when there's a bountiful dessert table nearby. Instead they grab the cream pies and let 'em fly.

Boy, do they let 'em fly.

No one's safe when the Stooges turn to dessert for defense. Butlers, hostesses, even royalty stand to be creamed by Stooge pies expertly flung across gilded rooms. Usually the Stooges are happy to serve up such sweet revenge. Except when the potential victim is a real lady.

Curly: You know, I quit my job at the bakery.

Southern belle: Why?

Curly: Oh, I got sick of the dough and thought I'd go on the loaf.

Uncivil Warriors

In *Half-Wits Holiday*, Moe is approached at a ritzy party by a friendly woman who inquires after his well-being. Not wanting to blow his cover as a gentleman, Moe disposes of the pie he's carrying by tossing it straight upward, where it sticks to the ceiling. The woman doesn't notice, but Moe is an expert when it comes to the composition and viscosity of pies; he knows that it won't be long before the dessert plummets down from its sticking place.

Naturally, this tentative state of affairs makes for uneasy conversation, and the woman notices Moe's fidgety discomfort.

"Young man," she remarks, "you act as if the sword of Damocles were hanging over your head!"

"Lady," Moe replies, "you must be psychic . . ."

Soon, the pie and the lady are one, a result Moe regrets despite the fact that he runs away.

Prepare this recipe for Sword of Damocles Triple Cream Pie only in kitchens with easy-to-clean ceilings, and away from the company of any true ladies you happen to know.

And take time to enjoy a bite or two before you let it fly.

• •

1 box (3.4 ounces) banana cream instant
pudding and pie filling mix

3 cups cold half-and-half

1 9-inch graham cracker pie crust

1 box (3.4 ounces) vanilla instant pudding and
pie filling mix

1 ripe banana, peeled and thinly sliced
(optional)

2 cups whipped topping

1. Combine the banana cream pudding mix and 1½ cups of the half-and-half in a bowl. Blend with an electric mixer on low speed for 2 minutes. Pour the pudding into the pie crust and refrigerate for about 1 hour until filling is set.

2. Combine the remaining 1½ cups half-and-half with the vanilla pudding mix in a bowl. Blend as before on low speed for 2 minutes. If desired, add a layer of sliced bananas to the chilled pie. Pour the vanilla pudding evenly over the banana filling and refrigerate pie until top layer is set, about 3 hours.

3. Cover the pie with whipped topping before serving.

Makes 8 servings

Chopper Kane's Out-of-Shape Creampuffs

Difficulty Level: Stoop

In the fitness age, it's easy to forget that some desserts achieve greatness precisely because they make you fat.

Take the nobel creampuff. Without this unassuming, high-calorie pastry, the Stooges might have been turned to mincemeat in the thrilling film *Fright Night*.

As trainers of ferocious boxer Chopper Kane, Moe, Larry, and Shemp slave to work their fighter into shape for his championship bout against Gorilla Watson. But after homicidal gangster Big Mike explains that Chopper must *lose* the fight, the Stooges stuff their man's gullet full of the most fattening food they know: creampuffs.

The plan works like a charm, and Chopper turns soft as a baby. But when girlfriend Kitty dumps him, Chopper again becomes terrible and vows to win the fight. This is not happy news for Big Mike, who promises to take the Stooges for a ride . . . a "one-way ride." The Stooges valiantly battle Big Mike and his gang of hoods, and emerge victorious by virtue of Shemp's facility with an ax. Lost in the commotion, however, is the simple creampuff, which did its plumping duty without complaint or fanfare.

• •

1 box (3.4 ounces) coconut cream instant
pudding and pie filling mix

1¾ cups cold milk

½ cup whipped topping

6 baked puff pastry shells

3 ounces caramel flavored sundae syrup

1. Combine the coconut cream pudding mix and the cold milk in a bowl. Blend with an electric mixer on low speed for 2 minutes. Refrigerate pudding for about 1 hour until set. Stir the whipped topping into the coconut cream filling. Keep chilled until ready to serve.

2. Use a fork to remove the tops of each pastry shell, pulling out the soft pastry underneath. If desired, set tops aside to use as a dessert garnish. Spoon the creamy filling into the hollow center of each shell, mounding tops slightly. Drizzle each creampuff with 1 tablespoon caramel syrup before serving.

Makes 6 servings

Always try to get every drop from bottles of food and drink.

Curly's Clumsy Tummy Ache Birthday Cake

Difficulty Level: Lug

The Stooges develop a messy relationship with birthday cake in their tour de force, *An Ache in Every Stake.*

First, Curly loses his grip on a gigantic block of ice he has lugged up a narrow outdoor staircase. A man carrying a scrumptious birthday cake at the bottom of the staircase winds up wishing he hadn't worn such a nice suit to the bakery that day.

> I baked a cake once, but it fell and killed a cat.
>
> Moe, in *Uncivil Warriors*

Next, after being hired to prepare dinner and dessert at a fancy home, the Stooges whip up a birthday cake to honor the man of the house . . . the same man who collided with Curly's block of ice. When Larry tests the cake for doneness by jabbing it with a fork, the cake deflates with a sorry "pssssttt." Moe's solution: jab a gas hose into the side of the cake, turn on the pressure, and "Pump in four more slices!"

With the cake gloriously reinflated, the Stooges present it to the guest of honor and sing this merry song (sung to the tune of "London Bridge"):

> *We baked you a birthday cake;*
> *If you get a tummy ache,*
> *And you moan and groan and woe,*
> *Don't forget we told you so!*

All looks swell until the man blows out the candles on his cake, an unwise decision whenever your birthday cake is composed mostly of flammable gas.

••

1 box (18¼ ounces) devil's food cake mix

⅓ cup sour cream

⅔ cup water

½ cup vegetable oil

3 eggs

1¾ cups cold milk

1 box (3.8 ounces) chocolate instant
pudding and pie filling mix

2 cans (16 ounces each) chocolate fudge frosting

1. Preheat oven to 350°F. Grease two 9-inch round cake pans
and set them aside.

2. Empty the contents of the cake mix box into a mixing bowl.
Combine the sour cream and water in a 2-cup liquid measure
and stir until well blended. Pour the mixture over the cake
mix, also adding the oil and the eggs. Blend with an electric
mixer on low speed until moistened, about 30 seconds. Beat
on medium speed for 2 minutes. Divide the batter equally
between the two cake pans.

3. Bake for about 30 minutes or until an inserted toothpick
comes out clean. Set the pans on wire racks to cool for 15
minutes. Remove cakes from pans to cool completely.

4. Meanwhile, pour the cold milk into a bowl. Add the pudding
mix and blend with an electric mixer on low speed for 2 minutes. Refrigerate pudding for about 1 hour until set.

5. To assemble the cake, spread half the chocolate pudding
evenly onto one layer of cake and cover it with the second
cake layer. (Eat the remaining pudding while finishing cake or
reserve in refrigerator for another use.) Frost the cake top and
sides with the fudge frosting.

6. Decorate the frosted chocolate cake with multicolored candy
decors and birthday candles.

Makes 12 servings

Moe's Six-Gun Seltzer Surprise

Difficulty Level: Baboon

Has the culinary world known a more glorious invention than the seltzer bottle?

As a weapon of self-defense, the seltzer bottle is unparalleled in its capacity to fend off meddlesome chefs, waiters, and other nosy kitchen pests. Watch Moe wield the bottle, and you'll understand why Larry and Curly give him plenty of cooking space.

As a dessert-making tool, the seltzer bottle plays maestro to a symphony of scintillating soda drinks, blasting vim into chocolate, effervescence into lime. Whenever the Stooges need to liven a limp drink, they summon the ever-faithful, tried and true seltzer bottle.

Not every dessert chef is willing to use the seltzer bottle. Certainly this is due not to the deliciousness of its contents, but to the difficulty of pointing the bottle in the proper direction. It is not the intention of this cookbook to be paternalistic, but anyone attempting a seltzer-based recipe ought first to study Stooge films—particularly those in which Moe is having a bad day—in order to fully understand the perils associated with using this remarkable tool.

Inspired by his seltzer marksmanship, Moe's Six-Gun Seltzer Surprise will be enjoyed by anyone who likes a little extra pizzazz in his desserts.

••

2 tablespoons chocolate syrup

¾ cup cold seltzer or club soda

2 dips (3 ounces each) vanilla ice cream

Whipped topping, as needed

Maraschino cherry

1. Pour the syrup into the bottom of a tall glass. Add the seltzer and stir to blend. Scoop the ice cream and drop into the chocolate mixture. Squirt with whipped topping and garnish with a cherry.

2. Serve the soda with a long spoon and a straw.

Makes 1 drink

Moe: I say, Jasper, how's your tapeworm?

Curly: Oh, fine. He took the blue ribbon at Madison Square Garden last week.

Moe: Fancy that.

Curly: *You* fancy that!

In the Sweet Pie and Pie

Marshmallow Gumbo

Difficulty Level: Mophead

What do you give three men who seem to have it all?

A delicious cake, of course. With marshmallows.

Serena Flint is grateful to the Stooges in *All Gummed Up*. Their miraculous fountain of youth potion has transformed the rickety old biddy into a ravishing young blond. Now sprightly and gay, Serena twirls to the front of the Stooge-owned Cut Throat Drug Store, intent on baking the Stooges a celebratory cake of marshmallows.

Serena, however, might have overestimated Shemp's facility for fetching ingredients. Instead of retrieving marshmallows, Shemp mistakenly provides bubble gum. Bubble gum is rarely a suitable substitute ingredient.

Soon, Serena and the Stooges are enjoying the cake, even if it does seem rather chewy. Serena reveals that this special dessert is known as Marshmallow Jumbo, to which Larry confides to Moe, "Tastes more like Marshmallow *Gumbo!*" Moments later, bubbles burst from everyone's lips, a lesson to aspiring chefs about keeping a safe distance in the kitchen between the marshmallows and the bubble gum.

••

1 box (18¼ ounces) yellow cake mix

1 can (12 ounces) evaporated milk

⅓ cup vegetable oil

3 eggs

1 can (12 ounces) red raspberry cake filling

1 jar (7½ ounces) marshmallow cream

12 ounces softened cream cheese

Miniature marshmallows, as needed

1. Preheat oven to 350°F. Grease two 9-inch round cake pans and set them aside.

2. Empty the contents of the cake mix box into a mixing bowl. Add the evaporated milk, oil, and eggs to the mix. Blend with an electric mixer on low speed until moistened, about 30 seconds. Beat on medium speed for 2 minutes. Divide the batter equally between the two cake pans.

3. Bake for about 30 minutes or until an inserted toothpick comes out clean. Set the pans on wire racks to cool for 15 minutes. Remove cakes from pans to cool completely.

4. To assemble the cake, spread the raspberry filling evenly onto one layer of cake and cover it with the second cake layer. Combine the marshmallow cream with the cream cheese in a bowl. Blend with an electric mixer on medium-low speed until smooth and creamy. Frost the cake top and sides with the marshmallow cream cheese frosting.

5. Decorate the frosted cake with miniature marshmallows.

Makes 12 servings

Stooge Songs to Cook By

Recipes will take you only so far.

If you really want to cook like Curly, you've gotta sing.

Research for this book proved that the recipes taste better if you sing during preparation. A double-blind experiment was conducted using the recipe for Cackle Soup. Three chefs prepared the dish according to the recipe contained herein. One remained silent, another repeated "The Rain in Spain Falls Mainly on the Plain," while the third gleefully sang Curly's famous high-pitched refrain, "She Was Bred in Old Kentucky, But She's Only a Crumb Up Here."

A panel of judges unanimously concluded that the third chef's soup was tastiest.

Subsequent tests proved that singing any of the Stooges' songs enhanced the flavor, texture, and appearance of the recipes in this book by up to $6\frac{7}{8}$ percent.

> ## "He don't smoke, drink, nor chew."
> Curly, disguised as lovely Irish lass Mrs. Dennis O'Toole, when asked by nosy Officer O'Halloran whether the baby he holds in *Mutts to You* is still on the bottle

Listed below are the words to many of the songs the Stooges sang best. Sing them loud and clear, and the rest is bon appétit!

"Adirondack"

This catchy ditty is used by Moe in *Boobs in Arms* to choose which Stooge will become the new boyfriend to a jilted woman. Cooks should use it to select between salt and pepper when confused.

> Adirondack one zell, two zell, three zell, zam!
> The bucktail thenaget tickle and tam;
> Eh, scram, the butcher man;
> See, saw, buck, out!

"The Farmer in the Dell"

This is the jubilant song sung to celebrate the Stooges' decision to become farmers in *The Yoke's on Me*. It is a fine general-purpose cooking song and works especially well for soups. It is sung to the tune of "The Farmer in the Dell," with Curly's joyous interjections in parentheses.

The farmer in the dell (onions!);
The farmer in the dell (potatoes!);
We'll make nice vegetables,
Like farmers in the dell (tomatoes!).

"Home on the Farm"

This yearning tune is sung by Shemp in *Gypped in the Penthouse*. Ideal for homey recipes such as Burned Toast and a Rotten Egg. It is sung to the tune of "Home on the Range."

> *Home, home on the farm;*
> *In Georgia our farm had such charm;*
> *And mama's so sweet,*
> *Cooks good things to eat,*
> *In Georgia down on the farm.*

"I Was Born in Brazil"

This tune was delightfully sung by Curly in *Sock-A-Bye Baby* while he whips up celery for a newfound baby. Can be sung effectively while preparing meats, fish, or fowl.

> *I was born in Brazil and I grew on a tree;*
> *When they shook the tree then I fell down;*
> *Then they put me in a bag,*
> *And they fastened on a tag,*
> *And they shipped me off to New York town.*

"La-lee, La-la-lee"

The premier general-purpose cooking song, written, performed, and immortalized by Curly, "La-lee, La-la-lee" may be sung or squealed delightfully while preparing any number of appetizers, soups, main dishes, and desserts. Simply fill your soul with glee, sing "La-lee, La-la-lee," and your recipes will burst with flavors tone-deaf cooks can only envy.

> **"You nearly talked us into buying ice, just to put on the fish!"**
> Larry to Curly, as the Stooges sell rotting fish from their fish truck in *Cookoo Cavaliers*

"Rock Caught Sea Bass"

With the vast selection of fish offered by the Stooges' fish truck in *Cookoo Cavaliers*, it's a wonder they're not still in business today. Perfect for fish dishes like Filet of Sole and Heel. Imagine Moe on lead vocals with Curly and Larry dancing in step.

Moe:	*We have rock caught sea bass;*
	Albacore and pickerool;
	Sand dab yellowtail;
	Tuna fish and mackerel;
	Bluefish, sailfish, half-and-half
	and if you wish,
	Swordfish, whitefish, herring, and
	gefilte fish!"
Curly and	
Larry:	*And that ain't all!*

"She Was Bred in Old Kentucky but She's Only a Crumb Up Here"

Perhaps Curly's greatest cooking song, "She Was Bred" was robustly performed over a juicy ham in *I Can Hardly Wait*. One of those rare numbers that can be spoken and still deliver flavor to a recipe, the tune is best sung at the highest possible register and with a maximum of squeak and warbling.

She was bred in old Kentucky,
But she's only a crumb up here.
She's knock-kneed and double jointed,
With a cauliflower ear.
Someday we shall be married;
And if vegetables get too dear,
I'll cut myself a nice big slice
Of her cauliflower ear
('Cause that ain't rationed!).

"So We Stuck Our Little Tootsies in the Water"

Short, sweet, and most appropriate for simple appetizers, the Stooges performed this little number in *Squareheads of the Round Table* and *Knutzy Knights*.

> *(A-one, a-two, a-three . . .)*
> *So we stuck our little tootsies in the water,*
> *And we ducked under the waves we did;*
> *Ha ha!*

"Way Down South in New York City"

Uplifting traditional tune sung by the Stooges in *Uncivil Warriors*, this song works best for urban-style meals such as Moe's Nerve Tonic and Panther Pilsner's Pie-Eyed Hot Dogs. It is sung to the tune of "Dixie."

> *Oh, way down south in New York City,*
> *The cotton grows on the trees so pretty.*
> *On the trees? On the trees!*
> *In the south? South Brooklyn!*
>
> *Oh, south of the Bronx where I was born,*
> *The songs are rotten and the jokes are corn.*
> *Look away, get away;*
> *Get a waitress; we're hungry!*

"The Wedding Bells"

This achingly romantic love song was warbled by the Stooges
to sweethearts Stella, Nella, and Bella in *Three Smart Saps*.
This is the perfect number to croon while preparing romantic
recipes for loved ones.

> *The wedding bells will start to ring;*
> *Ding dong ding!*
> *The birdies, they will start to swing;*
> *Ding dong ding!*
> *The bride and groom will start to swing;*
> *Oh, swing;*
> *So swing it!*

"We Just Stopped In to Say Hello"

Originally sung by the Stooges in ringing three-part harmony
while auditioning for talent agent Manny Weeks in *Gents
Without Cents*, the song is tailor-made for chefs who plan to
surprise a loved one with a hot home-cooked meal.

> *We didn't come to borrow any money;*
> *We didn't come to borrow any dough;*
> *We didn't come to borrow any trouble;*
> *We just dropped in to say hello.*
>
> *Hello to you, Mr. Manny;*
> *Please don't think that we are hammy;*
> *We just dropped in from Alabamy;*
> *We just dropped in to say hello.*

"Yankee Noodle Soup"

Most Stooge fans believe that "Yankee Noodle Soup" can be sung only while preparing Yankee Noodle Soup. What a tragic misconception. The song works wonders for any soup, including complex recipes such as Cedric the Clam's Clam Chowder. It is sung to the tune of "Yankee Doodle Dandy."

> *Our Yankee Noodle Soup is good;*
> *You'll find it is no phony;*
> *If you don't care for noodle soup,*
> *We'll serve you macaroni!*

"You'll Never Know"

Here is the Stooges' song of choice for melancholy occasions; it's perfect for those times when a recipe just won't go your way.

> *You'll never know*
> *Just what tears are*
> *Till you cry,*
> *Like you made me cry.*

"Don't you know it's bad etiquette to reach in front of a person when said person is trying to snag a morsel of food?"

Moe, before slapping a pushy Larry
in *Violent is the Word for Curly*

Moe is about to make a fruit salad.

"Zee Lollipop"

This joyous tune was recited by the Stooges to celebrate their lives as Parisian artists in *Wee Wee Monsieur*. It's ideal for the preparation of exotic foreign dishes such as French Toast from the Rue de Schlemiel and Joe Strubachincoscow's Moscow Latkes.

Zee lollipop, zee lollipop;
Zee la-la-la lollipop;
Woo-woo!

Zee lollipop, zee lollipop;
Zee la-la-la lollipop;
Woo-woo!

Zee Frenchman knows just what to eat;
He eats something so nice and sweet!

Zee lollipop, zee lollipop;
Zee la-la-la lollipop;
Woo-woo!

Index

About the Author

Robert Kurson is a 1990 graduate of Harvard Law School and is a Phi Beta Kappa graduate of the University of Wisconsin. He is currently a features writer for the *Chicago Sun-Times* and is the author of *The Official Three Stooges Encyclopedia*.

Since his fifth birthday, Kurson has nurtured a love for the antics and language of the Three Stooges. Grade-school teachers were baffled by his rendition of "Niagara Falls," a turn-of-the-century vaudeville routine popularized by Moe, Larry, and Curly in the film *Gents Without Cents*. He is a master of preparing Fillet of Sole and Heel.

Kurson was born and raised in Chicago and currently resides there with his wife.